Playing-Working-Growing

Temple Smith
London

Playing
Working
Growing

GEOFFREY IVIMEY

First published in Great Britain 1974
by Maurice Temple Smith Ltd
37 Great Russell Street, London WC1
© 1974 Geoffrey Ivimey
ISBN 0 8511 7062 5
Printed in Great Britain by
Billing & Sons Ltd, Guildford and London

Contents

To Jane and Andrew

It is not surprising that early opportunities for development have loomed so large in our recent understanding of human mental growth. The importance of early experience is only dimly sensed today. The evidence from animal studies indicates that virtually irreversible deficits can be produced in mammals by depriving them of opportunities that challenge their nascent capacities. In the last few years there have been reports showing the crippling effect of deprived human environments, as well as indications that 'replacement therapies' can be of considerable success, even at an age on the edge of adolescence. The principal deficits appear to be linguistic in the broadest sense — the lack of opportunity to share in dialogue, to have occasion for paraphrase, to internalise speech as a vehicle of thought.

Jerome Bruner, *Toward a Theory of Instruction*

Introduction

Almost every educationist and expert in child development agrees that early education is of the highest importance for children and that we need more nursery education, especially for socially disadvantaged children. On the other hand nearly every controlled investigation has shown that the early education of young children *as currently practised* has little lasting effect, and may even be a complete failure. Research evidence suggests that, although nursery education has an immediate effect on children who experience it, by the age of eight or nine other children from similar home backgrounds and of similar intelligence who have had no pre-school education have, in general, caught up. In the United States most experts have come to accept that the various remedial programmes such as 'Operation Headstart' have failed. The usual reasons advanced to explain this failure are that what was done was too little and too late: remedial education must begin early and go on for a long time if it is to have any lasting effect.

This is undoubtedly true, but evidence is increasingly being found to show that it is the kind of education, and the kinds of things teachers do that is at least and perhaps even more important. This is not to suggest that teachers are not doing their jobs in the best way they know. It does suggest that we need to look carefully at some of the assumptions and beliefs that teachers have and that influence their practices.

Most current thinking about pre-school education is dominated by the twin ideas of 'free play' and 'creativity'. Teachers feel that any form of interference in free play activity will stifle the creative potential of their pupils. This view derives in part from a misunderstanding of certain psychoanalytical ideas first advanced by Sigmund Freud, and in part from a superficial observation of adult creativity.

During the creative act it is probably true that the artist, writer or musician needs absolute freedom to follow out his developing ideas. But to assume that freedom alone is sufficient for this is to ignore the fact that most artists spend years acquiring and developing the skills necessary for the expression of their ideas. Freedom will result in creative acts only if it grows out of skills, knowledge and lengthy practice.

Freud's original insight into the value of freedom, especially of emotional freedom, was a valuable corrective to the over-repressive harshness of much of nineteenth-century childhood in Western Europe. His ideas were taken up and enthusiastically developed by people like Susan Isaacs who founded a successful school for young children in Cambridge. Children were allowed to grow in freedom, to develop creative ideas and to work through their fantasies and fears in play. It became apparent that creativity was closely linked with emotional spontaneity and freedom. Here, it was felt, was clear evidence of the correctness of Freud's views, and this discovery has become part of the conventional wisdom of mid-twentieth-century educational circles. Unfortunately, as with the question of adult creativity, this discovery ignored one fundamental factor. The children in Susan Isaacs' nursery school were almost all of high intelligence. They came, moreover, from highly literate and often very creative families. Their parents were for the most part professionally and financially successful. The children spent much of their early days in an atmosphere of books, discussion and creative thinking and were encouraged by their parents to value these things. The parents had not grown overnight into this privileged position of independence, wealth and freedom of creative thinking. Most had spent at least twenty years getting there, years that were spent in hard study, and for those who were university lecturers their period of study had probably never ended. To imagine that methods that 'worked' with these children would work unchanged with all children was surprisingly naive.

We can see therefore that the idea of creativity deriving from freedom is a gross over-simplification of reality. Freedom is necessary, but it is not sufficient to achieve creative activtity. Self-discipline, knowledge and practice are also important, as are attitudes towards individual work and literacy, and assumptions about what life is all about. Modern pre-school educators have seized upon the original insight while ngelecting the other essential requirements, and it is not surprising that *as it is practised today* early childhood education seems to have little lasting effect on most children. If we are to justify the vast amounts of time and money that will be needed to set up a properly functioning pre-school educational system then teachers will need to play a much more active part in the actual development of their pupils. This will not stifle creative urges. On the contrary it may very well foster them. This book has been written in the hope that the suggestions it contains will help teachers, parents and playgroup leaders to play this very necessary and more active part more effectively.

1 The meaning of play

In primitive and pre-industrial societies children occupy a clearly defined social position. Certain things are expected of them, usually depending on their age and sex, and they are accorded certain rights. They usually participate intimately in the day-to-day life of their elders and, as a result, they gradually absorb the beliefs, customs, habits and attitudes of their family, caste, tribe and people. They also gain some insight into the range of adult occupations that will open to them as they grow into their future adult roles. Little girls may help their mothers with domestic activities: weaving, gardening, cooking, poultry-keeping, collecting and preserving food, or whatever is locally important. Little boys practise bodily skills that will be useful to them later on as hunters, or they may even practise hunting itself, using real, scaled-down weapons to shoot small game. Among some tribes of the North American Plains Indians a small boy who brought home a bird or rodent that he had shot during this play-practising was praised as an adult would be. He was called a great hunter and his contribution to the family meal was respected as an adult's. His hunting was play, but it was meaningful play that helped him to prepare for the responsibilities and rewards of later life.

In other communities boys may experience an ever-widening range of agricultural jobs: crow-scaring, caring for animals, tools and so on. Two authorities who have studied children growing up in other cultures give us the following description of life in an African community:

As he grows older, he is given more and more chores to do for the family. He is asked to get water from the river, to bring wood, to feed the fire, to sweep out the hut, to hoe grass from around the hut, and to help on the farm. The first task of the young boy or girl on the farm is to chase

away rice birds, the small weaver birds who eat so much of
the crop. At a later age he is required to help weed the
rice, and then to help harvest it. As he grows he is called
on to share in more of the tasks of adult life — housebuilding, cutting bush, and clearing a trail, if he is a boy; or
beating rice, planting a farm, and cooking food, in the case
of a girl.

Gradually the child is inducted into the full life of an
adult. He is almost never told what to do in an explicit,
verbal or abstract manner. He is expected to watch,
learning by imitation and repetition. Education is concrete
and nonverbal, concerned with practical activity, not
abstract generalization. There are never lectures on
farming, housebuilding or weaving. The child spends all his
days watching until at some point he is told to join in the
activity. If he makes a mistake he is simply told to try
again. He is not punished for mistakes, unless he wilfully
rebels against the traditional procedure, or if the error is
costly. (J. Gay and M. Cole, *The New Mathematics and an
Old Culture: a Study of Learning among the Kpelle of
Liberia*, Holt, Rinehart and Winston, New York, 1967.)

At the same time children take part in the tribal and
family rituals associated with birth, death, marriage, puberty
and religion, and thus they come to absorb a whole range of
moral attitudes and assumptions. These are often unform-
alized but may be made explicit during special rites at the
onset of puberty. In modern societies most children are cut
off from much of this experience and we have to supply a
poor substitute by giving specific instruction in sex, extra
help in accepting death, and so on.

The children in these pre-industrial societies thus play a
full and recognised part in the life of their families and
communities. Childhood, adolescence and adulthood form a
unity. The young contribute to the life of their community
and absorb its *mores* (that is, the accepted values, expectations and customs). This persisted into the early days of the
Industrial Revolution in western Europe and North America
when little children, some only four years old, often worked
long hours in coal mines and factories. Their families had

simply transferred assumptions about childhood, developed in one set of conditions, into the new circumstances. Quite rightly people's consciences were affronted at this: factories and mines were no place for young children to spend their lives. Long hours amidst the noise, dirt and danger of industrial production damaged health and stunted minds and bodies. Humane and humanitarian laws were enacted to exclude young children from the mines and factories. In general they were successful and the children benefited immensely. But the legislation had the unforeseen result that children were cut off from the everyday life, activities and interests of their parents. As society has changed still further from its former, pre-industrial state this divorce between old and young has contributed much to the so-called generation gap across which children and parents contemplate each other in bafflement and alarm.

Families also began to change in other most important functions, especially in the areas of mutual support and early education and socialisation. These changes are by no means complete at present. In some ways young children are being pushed out of the mainstream of life: they may be seen as important in themselves as individuals and may receive very high standards of physical care, but both parents and children may be remarkably ignorant of each others' problems. This is reflected in the growth of specialised child care services: teachers, social workers, educational psychologists, youth employment officers, experts in sex education and so on, all helping to explain the young to the old and trying to help them to fit more easily into contemporary society. However necessary these people may be and however well they may do their work, they are esssentially *strangers*. They are not concerned with the totality of the child's life. They intervene, usually when some problem has reached critical proportions. They diagnose the problem and prescribe a course of action. In a few cases they may actually stay around long enough to see whether their advice was right, but more usually they disappear, leaving the parents to get on with the job of bringing up their children. But all too frequently the kind of life that many parents lead, and the education they had, do not fit them to help their children to best advantage. Moreover the growth of a body of 'experts' seems to have made many parents and teachers lose faith in themselves, in their knowledge, intuitions and humanity: they become increasingly uncertain as to what they ought to do. This process seems to be spreading: parents used to care for their children at least for the first five years of life. But now there is a growing movement to provide nursery schools at ever earlier ages. Nursery schools can be very useful in many ways to young children, but if parents come to see them (together with the playgroups that are springing up) as removing from them still further the responsibility for the care of their young children it is likely that we are storing up trouble for ourselves and for society in the future.

It has been noticed frequently that rural children, especially the *real* rural children, that is, those whose parents work locally, tend to be less often in trouble than their urban peers. There is less crime and vandalism in the country. Now there are undoubtedly many reasons for this: opportunities may be fewer, neighbours tend to keep a closer eye on each other with a view to gossip, in small communities everyone knows everyone else. All these are valid reasons, but what is often overlooked is that rural children are usually less cut off from their parents. Farm boys and girls may begin to drive tractors at quite an early age, or they may help with caring for animals and so on: they are more intimately part of the local and family life. Many urban children, on the other hand, even in adolescence have very little idea of the sort of work that their fathers do.

In earlier days and in technologically less advanced societies the play of children was often more like that of their parents: it was often recreational and occurred as part of a community activity (fairs, festivals, etc.) Today for children play has become the whole of life, except in so far as a child may be given some responsibility for a domestic chore. No longer is play a recreation from the serious work of growing and living in a community: it has become central to life. Many adults do not fully understand this change. For them play is still recreational, a valued change from the noise and bustle of earning a living. When they hear about and see children playing in nursery and infants' classes they often regard it as little more than 'mucking about'. Now a lot of play *is* mucking about, and this is not necessarily a bad thing because only in this way can little children experiment with their environment and learn, for example, what can be done with different materials, when to share their toys and when to assert themselves, how to express their fears and excitements symbolically and so on. This basically educational 'mucking about' is often messy, noisy and destructive, and modern standards of housing and furnishing, especially in blocks of flats, may make it impossible. We cannot blame parents: they have worked hard to build a pleasant home, their furniture may be expensive and not yet paid for, and they do not want it damaged or destroyed. But their children may be thrown back on watching the television by the hour or they may be given glossy and expensive toys of little real educational value (because little can be done with them except using them in stereotyped and repetitive games).

Even the most unimaginative negative 'mucking about' is probably not entirely useless: children seem to learn many things even in the most unsatisfactory of surroundings. But the pace of modern life accelerates generation by generation, almost year by year. Children in infants' classes are doing things that were once reserved for undergraduates (in the Middle Ages many scholars did not learn multiplication until they went to a university). Of course they may not be doing these things at the same level of sophistication or in the same rigorous intellectual way. None the less they are coping with the same difficult ideas. 'Mucking about' or undirected play depends a lot on trial and error and this consumes a great deal of time. Indeed in some situations children may never encounter the opportunities that allow them to develop skills and attitudes that are becoming increasingly important in modern life, especially the habits of mind and set of assumptions that underlie a scientific view of life. In order to be able to cope with the new mathematical ideas they will meet in a good infants' school, in order to learn to read easily and quickly, in order to learn how to get on harmoniously with other people they will meet in and out of school, children need a good deal of early experience. No longer is it sufficient to let these experiences come about by chance. We

must make sure that the children enjoy the right experiences
at the right time. We must structure their experience so that
they can get on with the most important of tasks, one that
human beings have evolved through the ages: the ability to
think, that is, to manipulate facts skilfully and symbolically
in the absence of concrete stimuli. This ability underlies all
advanced human activity: science, literature, art, music,
social relations, the development of language and, perhaps,
even of basic intelligence. This ability depends in part on
inherited factors, but it also depends (to a much greater
extent that many people realise) on what we experience and
learn. It is a skill, and like all other skills it can be improved
with practice or can become rusty with disuse.

Some interesting indirect evidence of this has come from
anthropological research in Africa. Important differences in
intellectual functioning have been found among different
tribes and these differences seem to arise from different
child-rearing and educational practices. One tribe discourages
original thinking in young people: the successful youth is the
one who can remember traditions and win an argument with
some slick wisecrack. Another tribe, on the contrary,
encourages its young children to solve problems and to think
things out for themselves.

In intelligence tests the young adults of the second tribe
perform just like young adults in Europe. In contrast in many
ways the young adults from the first tribe seem to be
imprisoned in ways of thinking similar to those of European
children. In particular they do not seem to progress beyond
the 'concrete operations' stage of intellectual functioning.
This term 'concrete operations' is used by psychologists to
describe the way in which children between about seven and
twelve years of age seem to think. These children can often
cope with a wide range of surprisingly sophisticated problems, but in order to do this they need something to handle
or something before their eyes. The same problems without
this 'concrete' help may baffle them. We adults are often in
much the same position when it comes to maths. A formula
leaves us cold and may even put us off, but an explanation
helps us to 'see' what it is all about. An example or two
worked in front of us, using simple figures, makes everything

clear. This simple example that we can actually see being worked out is 'concrete'. We can 'grasp' it.

Between these two tribes described there appear to be no marked differences of general culture, technology or genetic inheritance. It cannot be argued that the tests used were invalid, since this would leave unexplained the similarities between the second tribe and Europeans. The differences in adult intellectual functioning seem to be due very largely to different child-rearing and educational practices.

In this chapter it has been argued that for most children in highly developed industrial and urban societies childhood cuts them off from much of the real everyday life of the communities in which they grow up. This was inevitable when their parents were engaging in heavy, dirty and wearisome industrial work. But modern industrial civilization is moving into a new stage. Technological advance is making brute force and muscle less important than in the past. The growth of consumer-orientated service occupations will demand increasing sensitivity and intuition. Intellectual and social skills are likely to become increasingly important in everyday life. Already it is mainly the poorly educated who find it difficult to obtain permanent and satisfying employment.

Formerly children were cut off from their parents because they lacked muscle. As intellect and sensitivity become more important it may be that we shall come once more to perceive a unity between children's occupations and those of their parents. The early education of children, if it is properly conceived and humanely carried out, may contribute to the reintegration of childhood into the mainstream of life. Childhood will no longer be divorced from the interests and activities of adults but will come to be seen as a very important period of direct preparation for full participation in them.

2 How children learn

Teaching and learning are very different processes. Often they are not even opposite aspects of the same process, although teachers and parents frequently overlook this very important point. How often, when we point out that a group of pupils appears not to know something, do we hear a teacher say, usually in outraged tones, 'But I *taught* it to them last week!' The teacher has 'taught', but one cannot automatically assume that the pupils have also 'learned'.

Teaching is an attempt to bring about a change in another person from the outside. Learning is a change in a person occurring from the inside. Of the two, learning is by far the more important, and in one very real sense no one can teach another person anything, if that person is unwilling or (more importantly) unprepared to learn. Whatever the teacher does, it is the other person who must do the learning; and if for whatever reason he does not do it, then the teacher has largely wasted her time.

Of course if we work hard enough and if we use various rewards and punishments, then we can force a child to learn something, if only to pretend to be 'good' in order to avoid further punishment. Most children learn at an early age to 'count' up to ten or so by *rote-learning* methods. Sometimes they get it right, more often they are wrong: 'One, two, three, four, six, nine, ten!' Not only are they wrong in the order in which they place the individual numbers, but they cannot link each number-name with the appropriate set of objects. The learning is unrelated to experience and largely meaningless. Again, lots of parents (or, more often, grandparents) 'teach' their young the alphabet. The children soon learn to reel off 'A, B, C, . . . X, Y, Z'. The parents are proud. What they do not realise is that the ability to repeat a simple collection of sounds has no meaning. No one would attempt to teach a young child the names of all the capitals of the world's countries. They could learn them, but what would be the use of it? In fact teaching the alphabet in this way may actually have a detrimental effect. To link the sound 'ay' to the symbol A or to a and so on may interfere very seriously with the later process of learning to read. Most children learn to do sums in this rote-learning way: they may do page after page of simple computations, getting them all 'right' but appearing to learn no real, meaningful maths in the process. Indeed this happened to most of us, and if we are honest we admit that we do not really understand maths, that we are afraid of anything other than adding up the simplest shopping list and so on. My experience in a teachers' training college suggests that, year after year, up to forty per cent of the students find it extremely difficult to calculate a simple average of ten or twelve digits. Many of them panic when even the simplest mathematical symbols are put in front of them. Recently I asked a class of qualified teachers who had returned to my university for advanced courses of study whether they really felt they understood maths at even a very low level. None of them said he did, yet all had passed the O-level examination in maths and two had the A-level qualification. But these teachers are among the ten per cent or so most intelligent people in the country and they have had one of the longest educations in the world. Obviously rote memorisation is pretty useless. Cynicism prompts one to suggest that it may have another very useful function: it keeps the class of children working hard and quietly. This is excellent for the professional reputation and promotion prospects of the teacher.

Learning involves taking something from the outside and making it part of yourself, or internalising it. Rote memorisation, which occupies much of our time in schools, means taking something from the outside world and adding it to ourselves *without affecting us in the least*. Take a glass. Fill it with water, then pour the water out again. The glass remains as it was before. This is rote memorisation. Real learning is like the explosion of an atomic bomb: what we end up with is very different from what was there before.

There is some connection between teaching and learning.

Teachers teach and many children learn, but the learning may not be due to any great extent to the actual teaching. Watching some classes one often gets the feeling that many of the children are learning in spite of the teacher, while a few are failing because of what she is doing. Teachers are so often immersed in their work that they forget that children learn even when they are not being 'taught'. It is difficult to explain why this should be so, but it is a fact that most young human beings, along with most young animals, seem to have a desire to master the surrounding world and a curiosity about its details. While some teachers ignore this fact, it has led others to over-emphasise the importance of freedom in education. Unfortunately many children appear to have had a lot of these exploring and mastery drives knocked out of them by the time they come to school. Of those who still have them at the age of five, a good proportion have them knocked out after they get to school, especially if they find themselves in a very formal traditional setting. When this has happened the good teacher tries to restore her pupils' confidence in themselves and in adults, and also tries to help the children re-acquire the skills necessary for satisfying their curiosity.

One of the most important aspects of learning is *motivation*: ensuring that the learner wants to learn and is prepared to do something about it. In the earliest days most children are dependent for much of their motivation on others: they do something because daddy says they must. Or they do it because it will please an admired teacher. Some do it because they want to avoid punishment. Probably all these motivators operate in all of us at different times, but the aim of teachers and parents must be to make each individual child independent of outside motivation so that he will keep on doing what may often be a very difficult task in the face of temptations to quit. Some people can do this, others cannot. How does this difference arise?

The first answer is that it does not appear to be something 'natural' that some of us are born with and others without. By and large it comes through our experiences, and these operate in two ways: *imitation* and *reinforcement*. Surprisingly often children do what they see their parents doing. If you want your child to learn to read, then you must show him that reading is an important, valued activity. You must have books around the house and spend some of your leisure time reading. It is amazing how often parents and teachers say that they want children to read. Yet the homes of these children may contain no books and, if the truth were known, some of the teachers themselves do not read much for pleasure. It is not surprising then that as these children grow up they come to realise that they have been conned: they have spent many hours of time and lots of energy learning to do something that the adults around them do not appear to value. With children what you *do* is more important than what you *say*.

Reinforcement is a rather technical term. In everyday words it means something that is pleasant. It may be a reward or just a smile or a pat on the back. Psychologists have discovered that if some action is followed closely by a reinforcer that action will tend to be repeated. If the child does something helpful and receives a smile and word of thanks, then he is likely to be helpful again. It is as though the smile and the thanks make him 'feel good' and, since we all like to feel good we tend to repeat those activities that bring about this desired end. Looked at from another point of view, if one action is regularly paired with pleasant feelings, when that action is repeated it will tend to revive inside us some of those pleasant feelings. In time we associate the activity with these pleasant feelings and it is at this point that our motivation has become free from dependence on outside influence. We are now autonomous and will carry on doing things because we 'like' them. The point is that this autonomy or independence is not something that we were given (or not given as the case may be) at birth: it grew steadily through many years of experiences that were first followed by or associated with rewards and reinforcements and that slowly became rewarding and reinforcing in themselves.

Actions will be repeated even in the absence of reinforcement and reward. But as time passes they will tend to become less frequent and may disappear altogether. In the words of psychologists the actions have been *extinguished*.

All too often parents and teachers take good behaviour for granted. The only sorts of activities that are noticed are the naughty ones, and these may be punished. Research has shown punishment to be a very poor means of changing behaviour unless it is quite savage and follows immediately on the undesired behaviour. It may stop some naughtiness but it has two undesirable side-effects. In the first place the person doing the punishing is being associated with something that is unpleasant. Gradually he may come to be seen as unpleasant in himself: no wonder many adults and adolescents do not like teachers and other authority figures! Worse still, if a child does something wrong we may punish him and this may prevent him from doing that thing again, but all too often there are hundreds of ways of doing things wrong and only one or two of doing them right. Punishment may block off one road but it still leaves many potentially wrong roads open. Reinforcement at least has the merit of indicating what is right and what bring the welcome 'feeling good'.

Incidentally, undesirable behaviour may be reinforced unintentionally. Babies are very good at doing this. When a baby cries his mother hurries along and picks him up. Being picked up is a powerful reinforcer for babies, so the baby is likely to cry again, even in the absence of some physical cause. When the mother picks up the baby he stops crying, and this stopping of a loud, persistent and unpleasant noise is reinforcing for the mother. As a result she is likely to hurry to pick the baby up again next time he cries. In this way the mother is actually 'teaching' her baby to cry more often, and the baby is 'teaching' his mother to pick him up quickly. One American woman psychologist decided to put this insight to good use. She picked her baby up a lot when he was comfortable and making 'happy noises'. As a result these happy noises were reinforced and became more frequent in the baby's repertoire of behaviour. Reports suggest that the other mothers in the street were jealous of this well-behaved baby, which was undoubtedly an additional reinforcer for the astute psychologist.

We have looked at an example of accidental mutual reinforcement that resulted in a certain kind of behaviour, in this case crying. Some other reinforcement may be more conscious and intentional. Especially in adolescence, a child's peers (fellow pupils, friends or members of the same gang) may reinforce actions that parents and teachers are trying to eradicate. A teenager may cheek his teachers, engage in acts of vandalism or minor crime. If he is caught he may be punished but his peers may give him their support and approval. Apparently in some circles to have 'done time' in gaol is seen as relatively honourable. If the approval of peers is seen as more important than the disapproval of adults, if it is seen as more powerful than any punishment that parents, teachers and police are likely to use, then the undesirable behaviour will be reinforced and it is likely to occur more frequently.

The lessons are obvious: if we want children to learn something we must make sure that it is pleasant and followed by a reinforcer. Let us look at reading again. It is probable that readers are made or marred long before they ever go to school. Some children regularly curl up on their father's or mother's lap for a 'read' or story just before they go to bed. What is happening here? They are learning new words and new ideas, certainly, but also reading is being associated with feelings of warmth, security and comfort. Other children who have not had these enjoyable experiences do not learn so much, and words, ideas and reading may not appear so pleasurable to them. It is hardly surprising therefore that they do not approach the very difficult task of learning to read with very much enthusiasm.

Of course, these methods do not yield immediate results. Reinforcements need to occur frequently before they begin to have much effect on the very complex human and social situation that we are considering. Children will not wish to imitate a teacher whom they do not know or do not trust but, given admired adult models to imitate and given regular encouragement and reinforcement, most children will grow from being dependent for their motivation on their teachers and parents towards a state of personal independence.

Now, having considered these very important points all too briefly, we must ask how do children, in fact, learn? First of all they are active: they must *do* something. They need to explore and manipulate. Many, but not all, adults can explore in their heads. Young children need to use their hands and bodies. Passive learning in terms of words that are not understood is useless. Indeed, it is worse than useless: not only do the children not learn anything, but they come to sense that the activities they are engaged in are meaningless. This realisation is likely to turn them off school and learning in other ways too.

Before we give the children words they must meet things and handle them. They must, through personal exploration, see what things can do and what not. They must explore shapes and textures. While this is going on they need to be immersed in language: this is where the teacher becomes important. Words linked with experiences enable the child, later, to relive those experiences through words and thought alone. He may have the experiences without the words: in this case his thinking remains at a low, concrete level for much longer than normal. Or he may have the words without the experiences. This may enable him to appear to know a lot, but his knowledge is very poorly based, like that of the teachers referred to earlier who, in spite of spending a long time learning maths, were unhappy with mathematical ideas and did not look at the world in any sort of mathematical way. Many of them were even unable to do simple computations.

Jean Piaget, the great Swiss psychologist, has shown how the most abstract adult thinking has its roots in the body movements and the sensory exploration of early infancy. He suggests that learning is rather like eating. We eat most keenly when we are hungry. The food is at first outside us. We take it in and digest it, but after we have finished digesting we are not the same as we were before. Our bodies are stronger or weaker, according to whether the food was of the right sort or not. Not only must the food be of the right sort, but our bodies must be able to digest it. A diet of chips and sausages would not be readily digestible by a new-born baby.

Learning is rather like this. At first the matter to be learned is outside us and we must 'hunger' for it; that is, we must be motivated to take it in. Then we assimilate it, and during the process of assimilation we are changed. Our minds accommodate to the new knowledge. Once something has been learned meaningfully and not merely on the level of rote memory, only accident or disease or perhaps very severe punishment and brain-washing can remove it. Our knowledge is like an invisible model of the world that we carry around inside us, Once we accommodate to new knowledge then our internal model changes. If the ideas contained in this book are new to you and you assimilate them so that you accommodate to them you will not be the same as you were before. You will look at children in different ways and you will treat them in different ways as well.

But this process of accommodation and assimilation is not automatic. If the ideas are too advanced for the learner then he will be unable to process them. Indeed there is some evidence that for him these difficult ideas simply do not exist. By rote-learning methods he may appear to grasp them, but they really remain outside him. When he no longer needs to please adults or when threat of punishment (say, after an examination) has receded he will forget them much more rapidly than he acquired them. The Russian psychologist Vygotsky urged teachers always to 'teach in the tomorrow of the child'. Do not waste time on teaching things he already knows, and do not waste time on things that he is far from ready for. Teach things that are just beyond his intellectual horizon and he will learn them very quickly. In other words there are some things that a child is ready to assimilate and that he can accommodate to. There are others that are so far distant that they do not exist for him. Of course, in order to do this, we must find out what each child is ready to learn and pay less attention to what we think he ought to be ready to learn.

Accommodation is totally different from rote memorisation. Rote learning is rather like heaping up a pile of bricks in a building lot. You throw on one brick, then another and another. The pile grows, but the addition of each brick does not alter the bricks that are already there; the small bricks do not become larger, nor the red bricks yellow. Accommodation is like the life of an insect. A caterpillar spins a cocoon, and eventually 'hatches out' as a butterfly. It is the *same* animal at every stage, but its appearance, functions and behaviour are totally different in each. With

human intellectual and emotional development what was
formerly confused may become as clear as day. What once
seemed rather obvious and clear may suddenly be seen to be
very difficult with all sorts of problems that before we could
not even guess at. Usually this process of accommodation
goes on without our being at all aware of it, but sometimes
the change is so great and sudden that we experience the
'Aha feeling'. Now we understand the world and look at it in
a new light. It is rather like falling in love with the girl (or
boy) next door. Until this moment you have known her (or
him) for years as a very ordinary sort of person. Suddenly the
whole world looks new and wonderful. It also brings a
number of new problems with it. Especially important is the
fact that we cannot look backwards to discover what life was
like before this wonderful moment. Our whole outlook has
changed.

It is this total restructuring of experience and outlook that
occurs several times between early childhood and adulthood
that makes us adults unaware of how our children really
think. I have carried out research and made demonstrations
to illustrate the non-adult thinking processes of young
children. I know what the results will be, yet everytime I am
surprised that it should be so. We will find out more about
this in the next chapter.

3 The intellectual development of children

Little children live in the same objective world as adults, but they often do not seem to see it in the same way. This is inevitable: we make sense of the world first of all by noticing regularly recurring features in it. We put them into sets of categories that we have built up on the basis of our experience, and we remember and use them to guide us in our subsequent contacts with the world. Sometimes we make mistakes: our memories may be faulty, or we may not perceive something clearly so that we misclassify it in some way. Or it may be that our previous experience has been insufficient for us to construct the correct internal 'model' of the world that we all carry around with us. In this last case any new data that we come across do not seem to make sense, or they do not fit in with what we believe to be true. When this happens many of us tend to ignore the new data.

Now small children have not had the opportunity to observe much: they have not been long enough in the world. In addition psychologists know that memory is not, on the whole, a set of skills which operates very efficiently in early childhood. To develop efficiently memory depends partly on increasing maturity and partly on gaining the opportunities to practise using it. So as a result of lack of experience, of poor memories and of other poorly developed psychological skills, it is not surprising that the internalised models of little children are so different from those of adults.

Some interesting experiments show the difference very clearly. One day I was talking to a boy of four and a half. We were making 'snakes' of plasticine. First I rolled my lump of plasticine into a long thin snake and asked my little friend to do the same. We agreed that it would not be fair if his snake was longer or shorter than mine. With a bit of extra rolling here and pinching off plasticine there, we ended up with two snakes equal in length.

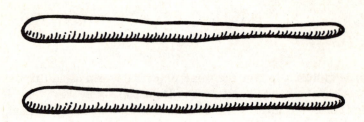

'Snakes' of plasticine

I asked my friend: 'Is my snake longer than yours? Or is yours longer than mine? Or are they both the same?' He looked carefully and replied, 'They're both the same long'. Then I moved the top snake a little to the left and asked the same questions.

'This one's longer'.

'No this one's longer'.

'I know. They're both longer'.

'Snakes' of plasticine

Pointing to the top snake he said: 'This one's longer'. Then he looked at the bottom snake and said: 'No, this one's longer'. A slight pause followed then he beamed happily and went on: 'I know. They're both longer.'

On another occasion I was demonstrating the points I am making now to some parents who were attending a Workers' Educational Association course in child development. One of the mothers brought along to one meeting her small daughter, about the same age as the boy mentioned above. She had brought her doll to the meeting too, for comfort and support no doubt. I had a bottle of lemonade and three glasses, two short and one tall and thin. Having established that both the girl and her doll liked lemonade I told them I was going to give them both some, and that in order to be fair we had to make sure that they each had the same amount. I nearly filled the doll's glass and asked the girl to tell me how much to put in her glass. With lots of comparing of heights of liquid, squinting with one eye, adding a drop here and another there, we at last achieved the desired result: two lots of lemonade that appeared equal in amount. I asked the girl: 'Now, have you got more than your dolly? Or has she got more than you? Or have you got the same?' She replied: 'We've both got the same'.

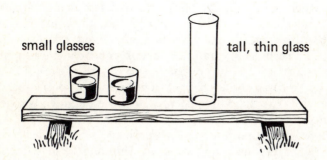

small glasses   tall, thin glass

Then I said: 'Now I'm going to pour your lemonade into this other glass, here. I must be careful, mustn't I? We don't want to spill any.' The little girl watched me carefully with a very serious face. Gradually her face changed: a beam of increased width spread over it.

'Now, who's got most? Have you got more than dolly or has dolly got more than you or have you both got the same?'

Happily she answered: 'I've got most'.

So I poured her lemonade back into its original glass. My friend looked less happy as she told me that now they had the same amount. She looked positively glum when I poured the doll's lemonade into the tall, thin glass and asked whether they now had the same amount. Very sadly she confessed that now dolly had more.

The doll's murder was averted by my pouring the lemonade back into its original glass thus reestablishing equality. The incident ended happily by the little girl drinking both glasses of the stuff.

These and many other experiments were invented and first used by the great Swiss psychologist, Jean Piaget, and they give us most valuable insights into the minds of small children. What was going on in the minds of the young children I have described? We do not know, but we can guess. Firstly they were using words in apparently the same ways as we adults. Yet suddenly we saw that the meanings of the words had changed: two things cannot both be longer than the other. One and the same glass of lemonade cannot be both more and less than another glass at the same time. For adults these words have some fairly fixed relationship to regularly recurring situations. Unless you do something to it, the amount of a liquid or the length of a ruler do not change simply because you change their shape or position. With these children the words seemed to have only the slenderest connection with reality.

More importantly than this, perhaps, we can see that the children could not separate their thinking from what they were seeing. Indeed they did not seem to see all relevant aspects of the situation at any one time. With the plasticine snakes the boy focused his attention first on one end: the top snake was longer. Then he changed his attention to the other end: the other snake now looked longer. He could not keep all the data in mind at once and therefore drew the wrong conclusions. In the same way the little girl was focusing on one dimension only – that of the height of the surface of the liquids. An older child or an adult would take into account also the changed cross-section of the glasses. In addition experience would have taught him that quantities do not change just because shapes do. But this takes a long time to learn.

Lest we feel superior and smug we should remember that adults often make the same mistake when judging relative volumes: many of us probably are fooled by manufacturers who alter the shapes and dimensions of packets to make us think that one contains more than the others. Even adults need a lot of experience before they stop believing the evidence of their eyes.

By using simple experiments like those described above psychologists have discovered a lot about the ways in which children think and the stages through which they pass as they approach adult ways of looking at the world. From birth up to roughly two years of age children are in the stage of *sensori-motor operations*. At this time the child's thinking is largely restricted to his perceptions and his physical movements. This seems a very simple sort of existence yet this stage is of the utmost importance: unless a child has a rich environment to perceive, and unless he can manipulate things at least part of the time, the signs are that his later intellectual functioning will suffer. Babies brought up in a Middle Eastern orphanage where the standard of physical care was comparatively good were found to be severely retarded, as compared with similar children living in normal families. The cause of the retardation seems to have been very largely a result of their early experiences. Each child was left for long hours every day in a cot whose sides were covered with white sheets, looking only at a featureless ceiling. These children were not ill-treated, indeed they received good care, but they were deprived of early stimulation..

One of the basic inborn features that characterises young animals, including humans, is curiosity: a desire to explore and manipulate the world. It probably has some evolutionary value: the animal that comes to know his environment better will tend to live longer, other things being equal. But it needs to be used if it is not to atrophy. Most young children have it, yet in some schools it appears to have disappeared by the time they grow into middle adolescence. One wonders what has destroyed this curiosity drive in the intervening period.

During this early period a small child gradually learns to coordinate the reflexes he is born with: sucking, tongue movements, swallowing, crying, gross bodily activity like kicking, grasping and so on. He learns to refine his initially crude physical responses to the environment, although this is a rather lengthy process: some children of even five years of age have little fine control over their fingers. More import-antly, perhaps, for his later development, the young child learns that things exist independently of himself. At first a baby behaves very much as though once an object disappears from view it has ceased to exist. In order to begin to understand the world, to begin constructing the all-important internal model that will later control our responses, we must learn that the world is a reasonably stable place, that it does not just stop when we close our eyes and that very little can actually be achieved by our simply wanting it to happen.

At about the age of two children begin to show that they have acquired the beginnings of the ability to symbolise. Gradually they are beginning to develop some autonomy of intellectual functioning, as their repertoire of habits extends and they start very hesitatingly to draw conclusions from what they experience and to generalise their responses to newer and more diverse situations. At this stage little children are very egocentric: they cannot look at the world from any position but their own. At the same time, in contrast to adults, they cannot examine their own thinking. They cannot retrace their train of thought to find any flaws in their reasoning. It is apparently this inability to examine their own thinking critically that results in responses like that of the boy who claimed that both snakes were longer than each other.

Around five or six years of age the cumulative effects of experience and practice begin to mould the child's internalised model of the universe. Sheer experience tells him that things do not change their quantities just because they change their shapes: the child is beginning to learn the principles of the conservation of volume, length, etc., and in experiments like those described at the beginning of this chapter these children begin to give the 'right' answers. When this happens it is interesting to probe a little more deeply. Thus a child might reply that the lemonade is still the same in quantity even though you have poured it into another glass. He is half way to achieving the important skill of conservation, but he is not there yet. If you ask him why it is still the same he may answer, 'Because you poured it', or 'Because it's orange'. He gives the right initial answer but he cannot say why he is right. It is as if he were guessing. Some children *do* give right answers and can go some way toward explaining them, but if the experimenter repeats the pouring, or whatever the test was, after a while the child breaks down and returns to an earlier way of responding, characteristic of younger children. These two sorts of response probably refer to two different stages of sophistication within this intuitive part of *pre-operational thinking*.

At about the age of seven (although we must remember that it is mental age rather than chronological or 'body' age that we are referring to here) children enter the stage of *concrete operations*. Now they can solve many problems that adults can handle. They know that the world is a pretty stable place. They know a lot about space and the location of objects within it, including the position of themselves within it as observers. They can begin to see things from the point of view of other people. What is more important is what they cannot do. They are not yet able to examine their own thinking, to go back over an argument to discover any flaw in their reasoning. In addition, although they can solve many fairly advanced problems they still need a lot of concrete help: they may still count on their fingers or need objects and pictures in front of them. (Many, perhaps most, adults remain in this stage for most of their lives when it comes to mathematics.) They can follow an argument if they have a specific example in front of them, but if they have to deal with a problem in words, or worse still in mathematical symbols, they are lost. This is just the position that many children find themselves in at school. They may be introduced to history (what adults did in the past), to exotic geography (what strange adults do in very different situations), to literature (often written by adults about adults and for adults in different places and times) and so on. The various problems are often dealt with abstractly: unknown phenomena are described in imprecise verbal terms. The sheer joy of satisfying curiosity, the desire to please teachers and parents may keep some children working hard and apparently learning a lot, but it is probably a sense of not really understanding that lays the foundations of a later rejection of school and its values in adolescence, exhibited in antisocial behaviour, lack of interest in school and so on. The need for concrete help in thinking and problem-solving suggests that at the ages of seven and eight children need teaching in the terms of the here and now: they should be learning about the 'geography' and 'history' of their own towns and families. They should be learning about themselves. Their maths and science should be concrete, involving handling things, looking at things, doing things, not merely learning verbal symbols about things.

I learned algebra at school and passed several examinations in maths. But it was not until I was in my early thirties that I really understood, for example, what $(x + y)^2$ meant, when I was watching some infants playing with structured maths apparatus in a good school. Many people, including many teachers of the older type, believe that if children play about they lose something. I am sure that many of these children could not 'say their tables', but they were getting to the heart of some real mathematical thinking. Learning the tables will come later, after the experience of things. Too many people have learned their maths and can say their tables, but do not think mathematically. The fundamental problem we should address ourselves to is this: not whether modern teaching methods are successful or not, but why traditional ones have, for most of the people who learned under them, been shown to fail.

With the onset of puberty children begin to be able to cope with the same sorts of intellectual problems as adults.

They are able to follow out arguments 'in their heads'. They can look at their own thinking — both processes and products — critically. They can argue by analogy and imagine things that do not exist. It is in this final stage of *formal operational thinking* that young people become interested in such activities as reading science fiction, attempting to solve the political problems of society, and so on. They may also be able to handle a much greater range of scientific and mathematical problems. Whereas earlier social rules and customs were seen as fixed and rigid in application, now they can see that circumstances must be taken into account. It is interesting to tell a story and ask questions as follows:

'Johnny was a little boy who was greedy. His mother had made some jam tarts and put them to cool on the top shelf of the pantry. Johnny wanted one so he took a stool, climbed up and stole a tart. When he was climbing down he knocked a cup off the shelf and broke it.

'There was another boy called George. His mother had put a tray of cups and saucers on a tray on a chair near the door. George rushed into the kitchen and the door knocked the tray off the chair, breaking all the cups and saucers.

'Now, who do you think was the naughtiest?'

Young children seem to have an absolute view of such matters: George broke more cups so he is naughtiest. Later, older children will take *motives* into account and perceive that Johnny was naughtiest, George merely careless or unlucky.

These differences more than any others, perhaps, reveal the intellectual gulf between young children and adults.

4 Play and intellectual development
I The foundations

'Do we provide the right kind of concrete experience during the early years? Do we provide at the same time language which helps efficient organisation of experience?' (Schools Council, *Mathematics in Primary Schools*, HMSO 1969, p.7).

Although the phrase 'intellectual development' involves more than the increasing ability to think in terms of mathematics, in this chapter our concern will largely be with the growth of the early stages of mathematical skills and concepts for two main reasons. First, we concentrate on maths because it sums up in the neatest form most of what we understand by intellecutal activity. This is:

noting regularities in our environment
classifying them
integrating them into a neat, elegant, unified system
drawing conclusions and making deductions from them
checking these deductions both in terms of the inner logic of the system and in terms of the relationship of the system with reality.

Secondly, we do this because of the increasing importance of maths, not only in the traditional sciences but also in the newer social sciences, in teaching, politics, geography, archaeology and so on. But we will see that 'maths' has very wide limits.

For most people outside schools today 'maths' still means sums. For many teachers, unfortunately, maths also means sums. We cannot sufficiently stress the point that sums are not maths. If maths and sums were identical then, for most of us, technological change would soon remove the need to do anything other than the simplest addition and subtraction. In my nearest supermarket the girl at the checkout desk has to do nothing but recognise the prices on the packages. She punches these into the till, pushes another button to arrive at the total and yet another to discover how much change to give me. She still has to count the change, but in other stores and on the London underground there are automatic change-givers.

If sums are not maths, what is? Many things involve maths. What, for example, is the relationship between smoking and lung cancer? Not every one who smokes dies of lung cancer, so how do doctors know of the relationship? How do opinion polls reach their conclusions? Why are they sometimes wrong and at other times surprisingly accurate, although only the opinions of a few thousand people are studied? What is the real long-term cost to us, as individuals and as a country, of joining the Common Market? Do pay rises put up prices? Why do we sometimes get more foreign currency for our pounds than we do at other times? These are obviously mathematical questions, although of course they involve more than just maths. Other problems that we solve every day involve maths of a very high order of complexity, and we usually do not realise it. For example, when we cross a busy street we function just like large computers: we must judge the distances and speeds of oncoming vehicles, the condition of the road surface, the speed that we can ourselves move, and to this we must add knowledge about the stopping distances of different vehicles and the probable habits of the drivers. We must do all this in a split second and make a decision as to whether it is safe to cross or not. It has been found that in strange environments, such as outer space, computers can make such decisions more efficiently and rapidly than astronauts. Clearly in arriving at a decision whether to launch ourselves across the High Street at rush hour experience plays a great part, but so does our ability to compute. It is not surprising that children often make the wrong decision and get hurt, even though they have practised their road-safety drill: they lack both the necessary experience and the computing ability to judge when it is really safe to cross, especially when (like their parents) they may be impatient and in a hurry.

The sort of maths involved in solving a problem like this one is obviously far removed from traditional school sums, but it is maths none the less. How then can we develop this 'wordless' (to us, at any rate) maths? It grows in much the same way as the more common 'word-full' and symbolic sums-type maths: 'Mathematical concepts have their origins in sensory experience of, and motor activity towards the outside world. But they soon become detachable from their origins . . .' (Richard R. Skemp *The Psychology of Learning Mathematics*, Pelican, 1971, p.39). Experience comes first then the mind-computer takes over and helps to free us from the need for experience. All too often teachers and parents want the computer to do its work before the necessary experience has been enjoyed.

The children in the best position are those who are given the opportunity to explore a rich and exciting environment and who have an adult (or several adults) around to talk about what they see and think, to point our similarities and differences in things, to ask questions and discuss answers. These lucky children form concepts by uniting many specific experiences. Gradually what is common to these individual experiences forces itself upon their attention; they learn what aspects are important and.what may (for the moment, at any rate) be ignored. These are the children who will later find maths and other learning at school much easier. Other children who have not been so fortunate may always find themselves baffled by many aspects of school and later adult life.

Let us take an example of what is meant here. Babies often spend a lot of time pushing and trying to push one object through another. Sometimes the thing goes through: there is a hole in the other thing, or it may be that the other thing is a non-solid, like the bath water. In the first case the baby is learning about shapes and space and comparative sizes, in the other about the properties of solids and liquids. It is common to see a baby trying to force one brick through another: he has not yet learned the differences between liquids and holes on the one hand and solids on the other. Because he has not acquired much language you cannot tell him about it, which is probably just as well. If you could he probably would not understand you. This kind of learning must be done on one's own. The experience comes first. The conclusions (that is, the concepts and knowledge) come later.

Thus intellectual development involves forming concepts 'inside ourselves' on the basis of preceding experience. At first our concepts are limited and concrete in nature. Gradually they become more and more elaborate. What was once tied firmly to concrete reality becomes symbolic. Our thought is freed from the shackles of things: we can imagine the impossible and follow complicated trains of thought 'in our heads'. This is called creativity; but the most creative people, the geniuses, inventors of radio, rocketry, the splitting of the atom, the discoverers of electricity and the theories of evolution all had to go through the early stages of sensory and motor exploration.

We have talked in very general terms about these early stages. Now we must look at them in the context of mathematical and intellectual development in much greater detail. The main argument of this book is that if we are to make our teaching efficient, to avoid too many false starts then we should do well to try to provide the right experience at the right times.

The earliest stage of intellectual development consists of learning about the basic nature of things. Children need to explore textures: the differences between smooth surfaces and rough ones, like the bark of trees, for instance. They need to experience the differences between stickiness oiliness, wetness and dryness. Little children often seem to find these basic sensory experiences fascinating. It is common during play to see small children stroking their faces with the long, smooth, nylon hair of a doll. I myself have a beard which seems to intrigue many children. Most of them will, if given the opportunity, give it a gentle tug to see whether it will come off or not, but many more will come and sit on my lap and shyly touch or stroke my beard, often rubbing their faces against it over and over again. Parents sometimes notice that little babies are fascinated with their own urine and faeces. They will touch them and finger them with none of the usual adult repugnance. There is no reason why they should not do this: these objects are, for them, like any others. If you can touch one, why not others, especially when they have come out of your own body?

Not only do children need to experiment with textures

but they need to learn the nature of things: some things will pour (like water and dry sand) others will not. They begin to learn the differences between fluids and solids. Then again babies may put sand in their mouth, only to spit it out again at once. Why should they do this, parents and teachers sometimes ask? A more important question is: why should they not? When they are thirsty they drink water or milk or pop. Sand is very like a fluid: it can be poured from one container into another. If you put it into a colander it runs out just like water. If you spill it on the floor it tends to spread out rather than to stay piled up in a heap. To the little child it seems very like a fluid, so why should he not try to quench his thirst and drink it? Far from being something strange it is the most natural thing to do. In addition it is a very sensible thing to do: many scientists earn big salaries doing just this: finding new substitutes for petrol, or butter, or natural fibres. Over and over again we shall be able to see little children behaving like scientists: they experience the world, they drawn conclusions and then they test them. Sometimes the tests work, at other times they are failures, but whether they work or not this form of building up our own supply of knowledge through trial and error is the real basis for all later intellectual activity.

One could go on multiplying the examples of experiences that children need: the experiences of comparing heavy and light objects, of big and small things, of things that float and those that sink. They cannot help but compare the heat of a summer's day with the delicious coldness of an ice-lolly or the water of a paddling pool, but it is surprising how few seem ever to have buried their faces in long grass and enjoyed its coolness on a hot day. Perhaps there is not much grass around in big towns and cities, and what there is is usually kept very tidy and short. There is very much to be said for keeping part of a garden or the grounds of a playgroup house or infants' school under long grass and bushes.

There are many useful little experiments that can be carried out without very much trouble. When it snows let the children try to catch the snow in their hands and watch it melt. Let them bring some snow into the classroom on a plate and put it next to some ice on another plate. Many children like to try to catch snow flakes in their mouths and are surprised that it melts and 'tastes like water'. (Incidentally, some are surprised that rain is water, too. For them, water comes out of taps!) When the teacher has talked about melting and freezing, it is natural to let a kettle boil and to let a saucer of water evaporate. In this way children learn that one object may appear in many different disguises: the teacher should not attempt to give a 'science' lesson. She should provide the situation, talk about it, teach new terms and point out the main facts. More importantly, she should encourage the children to talk, and then she may safely leave the learning to her pupils.

Most children experience these things anyway, whether they go to nursery school or playgroup or not, so what is so special about them? Why do teachers and psychologists emphasise them so much? Why not just let them happen? There is much to be said for this point of view: children must experience these things for themselves. The danger of a teacher or parent being around is that the experience may not be so spontaneous: it may begin to look like a lesson. On the other hand it would probably surprise many adults to discover how much that we think is happening does not, in fact, occur. The child may not notice it, he may not understand it, and because he does not understand it he may ignore it, thus losing a potentially very valuable experience. An adult can make a passing reference to the incident drawing the child's attention to it but not laying too much stress on it. Again it is vitally important that words be linked with every new experience. In part this is because this is the only way in which a child can extend his knowledge of his mother tongue, but it is also because, when he has linked words with his perceptions on a number of occasions, later the words alone will revive part of his experience at that time. These parts of revived experience we usually call 'ideas'. Many children born severely deaf who have not had the necessary opportunities to link words with experiences grow up with limited ranges of ideas: their thinking is impoverished because they lack the ability to symbolise their experiences. But there is an even more basic reason why language should be linked to experience. Psychologists do not know why it should be so, but children can learn things faster and more efficiently when words are used than when they are not. It may be that words attract attention or that words are linked in their experience with people and thus add some element of human warmth to things. Whatever the reason, the message is plain: experiences need words to be attached to them and it is mainly adults who can supply these words.

When little children are enjoying these fundamental primary experiences, at first they seem to see them as absolute: children are small, grown-ups are big. Children go to school, grown-ups do not. Most young children find it difficult to understand that student teachers have their own teachers. When they have a student on teaching practice in their class and the student's tutor walks in they simply cannot conceive of this new situation. Instead they categorise it in terms they can understand: the tutor is the father or husband or boyfriend of the student. Such a procedure causes much amusement among adults, but it is incidents like this that give the sensitive teacher and parent an insight into the working of the child's mind. It is things like this that show us the urgent need for talking about human relationships with small children: they come to accept the relativity of much of life gradually through experience and conversation. Of course, even when they come to accept that a grown-up may have a teacher of her own, they still tend to think of this situation in their own terms: the relationship between tutor and student must be the same as between teacher and young child.

Such a view does not altogether disappear even in later life: many young students when they first go to college or university still see the system of staff—student interrelationships as fundamentally the same as that they experienced in school, or even within their own families. Perhaps even more serious than this rather trivial example is the realisation (unfortunately missed by many teachers) that other more complex relationships will be misunderstood by their pupils as well. Such misunderstandings come from lack of experience and sheer misunderstanding of a lot of what the teacher says. Teachers talk and children listen: but it is wrong to imagine that they therefore understand. Not only do they not understand but they often do not even realise that they do not understand. All of this leads us to the inescapable conclusions: children need, more than anything else, abundant opportunity to experience the world of things and people and they need a skilled and sensitive guide to help them find their way through the thickets of confusion that beset their path.

How should a teacher or parent set about this important but delicate task? In part, just by being around and being prepared to make comments, give praise and offer advice. Yet this is one of the most difficult things to do properly. Beginners often talk too much or alternatively withdraw too much, leaving the child to his own devices. Little direct advice can be given in this matter: it is basically a question of sensitivity. Usually very little is needed beyond a brief comment: 'That's lovely, Janet, you filled that very carefully, right up to the top.' This may appear trivial to an adult, but little Janet may never have achieved this feat before and is probably very proud of it. It also requires considerable steadiness of eye and hand: something that all small children have to practice. Or again, when a boy has been experimenting with filling up plastic cups of different sizes with sand, it may be appropriate to step in and ask, 'Well, John, how many of those yellow cups make one of these big red ones, I wonder? Let's try together.' The teacher helps John to count, thereby linking the number symbols with real activity. Again, John is gaining experience in controlling his hands and eyes, and he is learning something about the nature of sand, especially as some of it will most probably end up on the floor underfoot and feel very gritty (an opportunity, here, for John to get a dust-pan and brush and help clean up afterwards!). Thereafter John can be left to his own devices and we may be sure that he will in the days to come return to his pouring and experimenting. In this way learning becomes a cooperative activity: the child does the basic things and the teacher keeps them going, intervening at critical points and then withdrawing again to leave the child to carry on.

So far, we have discussed intellectual development more or less in a vacuum. A major problem for beginning teachers and play-group leaders is how they are to provide the children with the necessary sensory experience in an informal way. In later life we do not usually think of art and maths or science as going together. This reflects rather our limitations than any real differences between these activities. Fortunately at this early stage we can bring them together again: one of the best ways of providing necessary experience for touching things and comparing them is in art activities.

Before embarking on a brief discussion of some useful art activities a word of warning is necessary: most artistic activity seems to be messy, but enthusiastic infants often throw themselves with adandon into whatever they are doing. The teacher who does not take this into account is likely to have a large number of rainbow-coloured children with paint and paste on their elbows, in their hair and behind their ears. This is not too serious and most parents accept it philosophically. In contrast mothers often get very annoyed when clothes are spoiled. Some form of covering is essential. and it should cover as much as possible. Small aprons are probably not sufficient. Much more useful are old shirts: each child should be provided with an old shirt of father's or of a big brother. These can be cut down to size and, when worn back-to-front and fastened at the back, they provide a very effective defence against the export of paint from school to home.

'A second word of warning is needed: art work with young children should be chunky. At this age children have great difficulty in controlling their fingers and even their hands, but they can execute big, smooth movements of their arms. They need large brushes, large sheets of paper, large pots of a few brightly coloured paints and of glue or paste.

Armed with these and safely covered by dad's old shirt, our nursery children are ready to begin. There are many different activities they can engage in. For example they can do *collage work*, sticking cloth of different colours and textures on to their paper to form interesting patterns and make pictures. The pictures probably won't look like anything we can recognize, but no matter. It is the activity of selecting and planning, of feeling the different textures and cutting the pieces of cloth up and then sticking them down that is important. Not only scraps of cloth may be used — any old junk can be pressed into service: toilet roll centres, egg boxes, pieces of string and wool, milk bottle tops, corrugated cardboard, embossed wallpaper (from old wallpaper sample books) and so on. Teachers of very young children seem to develop a hoarding instinct: nothing is ever thrown away at home, and every classroom should have its junk box or boxes to which the children can go when they are looking for some material to complete a picture.

Other forms of collage work utilise natural objects such as leaves and bark, wisps of straw, gravel and sawdust. The leaves and bark can be stuck on to the paper in the same way as the cloth and cardboard but the gravel, shells and sawdust can be used in other interesting ways: let the children 'write' on the paper with glue or paste, or let them try to 'paint' a picture with it. Then, before the paste dries, sprinkle on the sawdust or gravel. Leave it for some time then pour off the surplus. The children' are often amazed and excited to discover their picture appearing in visible form.

Another most useful activity is *finger-painting*. For this the children need large sheets of paper and vast quantities of paste mixed with poster-colour paint powder. The coloured mixture is spread thickly over the paper and the children trace criss-cross wavy patterns with their fingers (and often their hands and elbows too!) After the paste has dried the results are often quite striking, although once more we must emphasise that it is not the results that are important, but the activity and sensory experience.

Probably no nursery or infants' class would be complete without some form of *plasticine* or *modelling clay*. Home-made dough is probably more useful, mainly on the grounds of health. It soon has to be thrown away, which is just as well: dirty hands (that often spend a lot of time on the floor) playing with plasticine can soon turn it into a smelly, unsavoury, unhygienic mess. Ordinary dough, mixed with a colouring such as cochineal, is a good substitute and much cheaper. Children will spend hours rolling snakes and making cakes out of the material. Some will try to make animals and people. They will not look much like animals or people, because the artists lack both the skill in their fingers and the necessary concepts, but the attempt is useful in itself. It is often useful too, to show the children how the clay and dough may be used to make *moulds*. Thereafter the children will experiment over and over again with finding things to imprint: pieces of nut-shell or horse chestnut spikes, nuts and bolts, old army badges and so on. Some attempt at permanency may be achieved by using plaster of paris or Keene's cement, although this will need more intervention from the teacher and should be introduced at a rather later stage.

In addition to these activities the children can do 'real' painting, once more using large sheets of paper spread out on the floor, big brushes that can be grasped in the hand and a few brightly coloured paints in large jars. Here again it is sometimes difficult to know what the paintings represent (if indeed they represent anything). There is some evidence that little children often do not set out to paint some specific thing. Instead they begin painting and what they produce suggests the name of a thing to them: a picture might be in turn a banana, an aeroplane and the sun. Of course, the children do sometimes set out to paint something specific: usually a house or person or bus. This is usually something important to them and may reflect a problem they are trying to solve: something they are trying to understand or that has caught their attention. Once again to the alert sensitive teacher the painting can give valuable clues about the ways in which the child is structuring his internal model of the world. Houses do not at first look much like actual houses and people are often just heads with arms and legs attached. This is not important at first. Greater accuracy will come later as the child gains experience and control over his hands. Along with this there is a steady increase in self-criticism: children come to realise that their efforts do not look very realistic. At this stage they begin to acquire stylistic conventions usually from copying other children, and this is probably the optimal time for the teacher to intervene, talking about the picture and possibly (if she has the skill and knowledge) making suggestions.

These different art activities need not all be produced at the same time. The children can be introduced to a new one.

They will experiment with it for some time, then it can be put away and another brought out. Later the children will want to return to the previous activities and the teacher may be surprised at the more advanced ways in which they approach them.

Every infants' and nursery class or playgroup should have *sand and water trays*. These can be bought commercially and are in galvanised steel with wheels for ease of movement. Effective substitutes can be made for playgroups without too much expense. Small disused children's baths can be very useful, but the water tray should ideally have a tap for emptying out the water. The best sort of tray is oblong, with low sides and at a height suitable for the children who will be using it. It should be on wheels or be easily portable so that it can be put outside in fine weather. The sand tray must be kept dry and should be supplied with scoops, ladles, old tins and plastic cups and measurers. Silver sand, which pours easily, is the best kind of sand to use. A water tray will be supplied with much the same sort of containers: pipes, sieves, jugs, etc. It is also useful to have lots of different floating objects as well as some that sink, so that the children can begin to build up ideas about floating. Especially important for the water tray is some kind of personal waterproof covering so that the children do not soak themselves. In summer this is less important because the children can often strip down to their pants when playing.

Other useful apparatus that should find its place in the class for young children is a plentiful supply of *bricks* and *blocks*. These can be home-made, from off-cuts obtained from timber yards, wood of square cross-section cut into different lengths, dowelling and so on. These bricks and blocks should be of different sizes, from those small enough to be grasped in one hand to those that can be piled up to make realistic mountains with exciting caves to hide in. Children also need lots of long thin planks of wood to build roads and bridges for their toy cars.

Children need to explore not only the outside world, but also their own inner world. They need to experience the joys and fears of climbing, the sense of achievement of climbing a little higher today than they did yesterday. They need some sort of *climbing frame* to go up and over, as well as something to crawl under. Parents and teachers are often worried that if their children climb up they may fall. Some falling is inevitable and probably does a great deal of good: the children learn to accept the odd knock. Very rarely will the children suffer serious damage at this age: they do not usually risk themselves beyond what they know they can do.

Once the child has begun to experience these basic facts about the world (and such experience should begin from the beginning of life) then he is able to start the long hard journey towards mathematical and scientific thinking. At this time there is a tendency to hurry the child along too quickly: to get him doing formal sums and formal reading just because he is in the school. In part this is inevitable: if a teacher is busy with her class all doing things that can be seen — doing pages of sums and holding reading books in their hands — then no one can say that she is not working. Unfortunately the more important things are invisible: none of us can see concepts forming and internal models gradually becoming more complex. If a teacher does what she should be doing, that is, helping the children to lay the foundations for their own personal models of the surrounding world, old-fashioned head teachers and parents may wonder whether she is really earning her pay!

Another problem is that many of us are not very imaginative or creative. We might be pretty good teachers or playgroup leaders but we seem to run out of new ideas to help our children move along towards the next stage of growth. This is not always a bad thing: young children are very conservative and return time and again to activities and toys that they like. There is no need to engage in a frenzied search for new 'gimmicks' like some low-grade television producer trying to wean his audience away from the rival channel. None the less we do need to find new 'wheezes' and alternative activities so that the children can increase their experiences while practising the same skills. Much can be learned from the classrooms of other teachers, and no one should be afraid of picking up new ideas from wherever they can be found. A new teacher or playgroup leader should not be afraid of asking a more experienced teacher what to do and why: most teachers are only too pleased to help. Everyone likes to be thought an expert in something!

However, there is need for other sources of ideas, and luckily this need has been, in part, met. One of the most useful sources of ideas is the Nursery Course, produced by 'Three-Four-Five' a firm that specialises in pre-school 'do-it-yourself' kits and books for parents and leaders of play- and nursery groups. (Addresses and further details are given in the Appendix) The designer is an experienced nursery teacher of great skill with a sound grasp of all that is best in modern educational thinking, who has decided to offer her insights and skills to others. The course that Three-Four-Five produce is full of interesting and stimulating activities for young children. With this course they will enjoy working through many and varied pre-number and pre-reading games. They will be able to lay the foundations of later meaningful work in social studies and they will have listened to and joined in singing nursery rhymes and stories. The course contains not only brightly coloured activity cards for children to make things and to draw, but records for listening to. Parents are not forgotten either: full and useful instructions and advice accompany every lesson.

Three-Four-Five is suitable for the youngest children. Still more ideas can be gained from the numerous books on the market, of which the most useful is probably by Michael Holt and Zoltan Dienes, *Let's Play Maths*. This is more specifically devoted to the development of mathematical concepts in children between the ages of four and seven years. Once again, as with the Three-Four-Five course, parents are not simply told what to do: they are told why it is necessary that it should be done. Parents may have full confidence in both these works: they are not based on mere theorising. All the ideas have been tried out on real, live children. The signs are that, through using them, the parents not only come to understand their children better, but they actually enjoy themselves immensely.

At a rather later stage there is a most valuable series of books from which many ideas can be gleaned. This series is published by the Nuffield Mathematics Project. These books are intended mainly for teachers but parents and playgroup leaders will find them a most valuable source of ideas that they can use at home. The authors emphasise that they are not to be slavishly followed, but must be regarded merely as guides and starting points for work and experience of a much wider kind.

Some parents and teachers may like to develop their knowledge of the many interesting topics that they will find in these publications. An interesting and easily available book by Richard Skemp is *The Psychology of Learning Mathematics*. Not only does this inform its readers of the basic reasons for much of the best in modern educational practice, but it is also a useful source of ideas for lessons and projects at every stage.

5 Play and intellectual development
II Growth

In Chapter 4 great emphasis was laid on informal learning: the child can learn a lot through playing with carefully chosen materials. At this time the teacher's main job is to present the materials in interesting and attractive ways and to supply essential language in order to guide the child through the experiences necessary for laying the foundations of later growth. As children grow older they need a rather more formal setting for this exploratory play-work. The reader should note that it is not *formal maths* with the traditional meaning of 'sums' that is being urged here. The sort of mathematical and pre-mathematical activities to be discussed should still appear to be exciting and informal sessions of exploration and play. But for the teacher they must be seen as part of a regular and developing structure and care must be taken to see that the child does not, through absence or inattention, miss some vital experience. It is unfortunate that the age from four to about six years is the time of peak illness for most children. Coming into close contact with large numbers of other children for the first time in their lives they are exposed to the numerous infections that periodically sweep through schools: mumps, chickenpox, colds, tummy upsets and so on. Absence at an early stage may be more critical than later on: a child loses very little of importance if, say, mumps in adolescence make him miss some details about the Court of the Star Chamber. But even a short absence when a group of children is being shown how to 'do' multiplication may influence the child's performance increasingly over later years. This consideration reinforces the emphasis that has been laid on an essentially individual approach to learning at this stage. If Jimmy misses something but is making progress at his own individual rate then the lack can fairly easily be remedied. If, on the other hand,

Jimmy is a member of a group, then he is likely to be expected to make progress with that group, and it may not always be convenient for the rest of the group to repeat something or mark time while Jimmy catches up. The group continues to make progress and Jimmy flounders.

What then is meant by a more formal setting? As the child begins to encounter more abstract situations these may necessitate sitting quietly at a table and doing work of some kind. This may be done entirely alone, while other children are doing other things, or there may be a group of children doing roughly similar things. While they are doing these the teacher or a helper may look on, giving a word of advice, praise or encouragement here, demonstrating something there and so on. At the end the teacher will talk about what the children have been doing, asking questions and encouraging the children to talk about their experiences and feelings.

Perhaps we may sum up the difference between this and the earlier stage of intellectual development in this way: earlier, the activity of the children was channelled through play, now it is through games. To play a game implies a more serious approach, with rules to be learned and followed and a lot of practice necessary for successful performance. Yet a game also implies enjoyment and involvement. These two strands can be brought together by having many interesting and colourful activities available, so that although the child is doing different things he is practising using the same perceptive and cognitive functions. This means that he is using his eyes and ears and then practising thinking about what he has observed in many different situations. Children learn by observing many different situations. Each situation is complex and has many individual features. But each one also contains some aspects that are rather like others. We say that different situations have several recurring features. The children observe these regularly appearing common features and abstract them from the experience as a whole. On the basis of what they have observed and abstracted they build for themselves a set of rules as to 'what always happens next' or 'what goes with what' and they use these rules to understand the world. Now no one can construct a rule on the basis of *one* experience. Within very broad limits the more experiences we enjoy the more efficient and accurate will be the rules we make to understand the experiences. For children experiences are best presented in the form of games. These games can be grouped under the headings of work in *sets*, *ordering* and *matching*. All work should progress in this order.

What is a *set*? Initially it is a group of objects having something in common. Later activities and operations can also be treated as sets. Examples are easy to find: thus *humans* form a set in contrast with *animals*, *plants* and *rocks*, each of which also forms a set. *Males* form a set, including men, boys, stallions and dogs, as opposed to *females* (women, girls, mares, bitches, etc.). The *mature* (men, women, horses, cows) form a third set opposed to the *immature* (boys, girls, foals, calves). Using sets, we can make additional groupings: a boy is a member of the *human*, *male* and *immature* sets, a bitch is a member of the *animal*, *female* and *mature* sets.

At other levels there are other sorts of set. Most of us have learned geography at school. When we learned regional geography we learned about different parts of the earth's surface, such as the southwest peninsula of Britain. This shares some features with parts of southern Ireland and Wales (they form elements of sets of specific climatic and geological features). It shares other features with parts of northwest France (they are both elements in sets of history and economic activity) and so on. What makes southwest Britain unique is the way in which all these different sets come together or *intersect*.

Usually we do not think consciously in this way, although it might help us to sort out some of our many personal, economic and political problems if we did. But thinking like this in sets lies at the basis of advanced thought in many different fields today, especially in maths, computer work and so on. It also forms the basis of counting and this apparently simple activity demands considerable prior experience in, among other things, working with sets. Thus to a young child two elephants, two flies and two railway tracks may not have much in common. In fact to a young child two flies may appear more similar to three flies than to two icecreams. What the icecreams, flies, elephants and railway tracks have in common is being elements of the set of *twos*, in which the twoness is more important than the flyness or elephantness. This needs to be learned and it takes time.

Teachers and schools do not usually have supplies of elephants, railway tracks and such like around. Instead they must use more everyday objects. Fortunately these abound and making a collection of them is often interesting in itself to children. Conkers and acorns can be had for the picking. Coloured bottle tops (especially from beer and lager bottles) can be brought from home. At first children should be allowed to play with objects that they have collected: they may make lines or 'trains' with them, use them for making shapes and pictures or build 'staircases' with them.

Children should be allowed to play
with objects they have collected

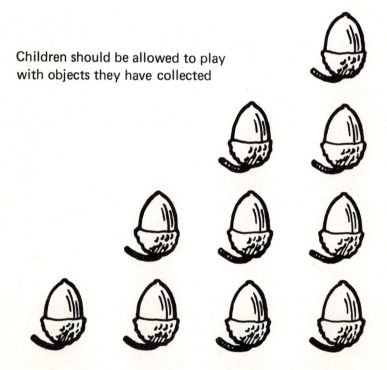

"Staircase" of acorns

Soon they will exhaust the possibilities of this play. Then is the time to step in and move the children on to a new stage. Sheets of paper with irregular hoops drawn on can be supplied, or real circles of string or wool provided. The children are given a mixed bag of objects and shown how to sort them into piles of 'the same things' — all the conkers in one pile and the acorns in another, all the red bottle tops here and the blue ones there. It often surprises teachers to discover how even such an apparently simple task can defeat little children at first. They need lots of practice and, with practice, it becomes easier.

At first the sorting should be rather crude with the discriminating characteristics very obvious. Later these differences can become more subtle and the sets that have been formed during the game can be used to increase vocabulary. In this way children can learn words and collective concepts like *tools*, *musical instruments*, *vegetables*, *cutlery*, *crockery* and so on. Of course even in the best supplied playgroup or nursery class there is a limit to the number of examples of things that we can have around the place. Catalogues and colour magazines may be used to provide large numbers of pictures of things that can be cut out. They should be stuck on cards and, preferably, covered with some sort of plastic to prevent soiling and undue wear and tear. Very soon a large collection of sets is built up and it takes very little time for the teacher to select examples from several and shuffle them together before giving them to the children.

Other activities can help the children to form more complex ideas: within one set the children can sort objects into big and little, round and square, and so on. The objects that are being sorted need not all be small enough to hold inside the hand: large and small boxes can be sorted into sets inside hula-hoops laid in the middle of the floor. The children need to sort and above all to talk about things that are big and small, heavy and light, long and short, fat and thin and so on.

At first the difference should be one dimensional. That is, when sorting objects into heavy and light, then the heavy things should also be larger and the light ones smaller. *Heavy small* things and *light big* ones are at first too difficult for small children. But later the games can be extended to cover these sorts of object. When this is happening children should be encouraged to guess which things are heavy and which light. Gradually they will begin to ignore appearance in favour of actual weight and in this way they will become able to sort out and use different concepts.

Sets of objects can take into account not only the objects themselves, but also their uses. Children can sort out things we wear from things we do not, things that are done at school and those that are done at home, things we eat at Christmas and things we eat on picnics, things we like and things we do not like. At this stage we have moved away from the individual type of activity to a group activity in which children explain their ideas to each other and to the teacher. Large numbers of new words can be learned and used. At this time too the children are introduced to new sorts of notation. Formerly the individual children made their own sets of objects inside loops of string or circles drawn on paper. Now they make communal sets of objects. If they are learning to read, cards with words written on them can be substituted for the original objects. Colourful graphs with cut-outs of sticky, coloured paper stuck on large sheets of squared paper can be introduced and should be discussed with the children. Thus the children are gradually introduced to common forms of mathematical notation.

We have already seen how children need to be introduced to sets of objects varying in two different ways at the same time: size and weight. They will need much practice in handling these and other two-dimensional problems. Many examples are given in Holt and Dienes' *Let's Play Maths*, and the imaginative teacher or parent will be able to invent many others. One useful game that can be made at home and that seems to capture the interest of children are 'felt families'. Big and little figures of men and women, boys and girls can be cut out of red and green felt. A set like this can be used in many ways: at first the children can sort them into males and females, or grown-ups and children, or reds and greens. Later they can sort them using two dimensions: small reds and large reds, small greens and large greens.

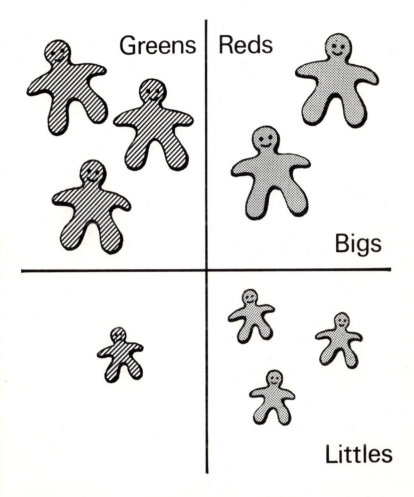

Greens | Reds

Bigs

Littles

Children need to be introduced to sets of objects varying in
two different ways at the same time
             big v little
             red v green

Gradually, through discussion and experiment, the children can be led to invent their own sub-classifications: males and females versus reds and greens; grown-ups and children versus greens and reds, and so on. Later still another dimension can be added. As well as sex, size and colour it is possible to distinguish between fat and thin figures. Children may go on then to see many other possible sets that can be formed.

In yet other kinds of set games the children themselves can be used as objects. They can find out how many of their classmates have pets of one kind or another, how many like watching 'Top of the Pops' and other television programmes, how many have their birthdays in each month and so on. Each of these activities is not only valuable in itself but also provides opportunities to talk and to learn new words and ways of looking at the world. And each activity leads naturally on to some practice in recording the results. This recording, in turn, naturally gives opportunities for practising reading and counting.

Many other natural objects can be pressed into use for this sort of game. Sticks can be collected on walks and during outside play periods. Long and short sticks can be contrasted with thick and thin. Big, little and medium stones can be sorted, as can red rosy apples and green ones. At this stage yet another stage of intellectual development has been entered. The objects that are being experimented with now cannot easily be sorted into only two classes: the children are dealing with objects that vary continuously along some dimenson. Biggest and smallest apples are relatively easy to classify, but the ones in the middle are more difficult: decisions have to be made. Perhaps a third class is needed: medium, or half-full and half-empty. This can lead on to many long discussions and arguments: what is medium? There is no answer and it is only through experience that children come to realise this: a glass that is half empty is the same as one that is half full. A small elephant is bigger than a large mouse. These points are not trivial. In the ancient world some of the best brains were defeated by trying to explain how an object could at one and the same time be large (like an elephant) and small (like a baby elephant compared with other elephants). For them largeness and smallness were fixed attributes. Like little children, they had not developed notions of relativity. Nor had they realised, again like little children, that names and descriptions are inventions of men: they have no objective reality in nature.

So far the sets that we have been discussing have all been of objects with common features. Many other sets are not like these: each object is different from each of the others but within the set they complement each other. Thus we have the set of cup-and-saucer or knife-fork-and-spoon. We have the set of a family: father-mother-sons-daughters, and perhaps granny or grandad and Spot the dog. Then again there are the sets of rooms we call a house, of chairs and tables we call furniture and so on.

As with the early kinds of experience discussed in Chapter 4, a very great problem here is the manner and timing of introducing new activities. Although the various sorts of activity should be introduced in the order in which they are described here (because each group of activities calls into operation higher levels of sophistication) the teacher must not go on from one activity to another in a mechanical way. Young children are conservative: they often like to stay with the things they know. In addition when we begin to learn something new and rather taxing it is often pleasant to return to something we can do relatively easily. It is as though when we meet a new problem that looks like defeating us it is reassuring to go back to something that we can do and thus reconvince ourselves of our own ability. The sensitive teacher will always make sure that earlier activities are readily available for revision. Sometimes they can be laid out on a side table. At other times the children can be asked what is their favourite activity, and so on.

Another reason why the activities described cannot be followed slavishly is that working with sets overlaps work with other activities. These may usefully be introduced among the earlier set-activities. In fact, as we have seen with the problem of the 'medium', the very problem of classifying objects in sets leads automatically and naturally on to the problem of *ordering*, or the sorting out of *relations* between similar objects. Here children must learn the relationships of equivalence or equality, of 'more than' and 'less than', of 'before' and 'after', etc. These relationships are not always easy to perceive even though we adults take them for granted. Let us examine what is implied in a sum, for example,

$$9 + 4 = 13$$

First, there is no obvious reason why the marks on each side of the 'equals' sign should be equal. They are equal only if we use a notation with a base of ten. Beyond this there is the problem of 'joining together' represented by '+'. Once more it has meaning only in a restricted context. Even quite small children may point out that to put one rabbit with another does not mean that one ends up with only two rabbits. Conversely if there are five flies on the table and I swat one, there is only one left: the dead one. The rest have flown away. But there are problems beyond these: the symbol '9' must be learned as representing the set of nine objects. Until this has been gained it is a meaningless squiggle. The same applies to '4' and '13'. This last one has an additional difficulty: the '1' does not equal 'one' but 'ten'. Underlying the simplest sum is a whole host of skills. Each must be mastered before the sum can really be 'understood'. It is possible to get a sum 'right' without any understanding.

If the child enjoys the experiences already described in this book he will be well on the way to mastering some of these skills. But because of the professional pressures that teachers are exposed to and because they have often forgotten the stages of their own early learning there is always a danger that they will hurry their pupils on to more formal work too quickly. But these early stages cannot and must not be hurried. Children *can* learn to manipulate symbols. Many will learn to complete the sum very quickly. Yet to what end? The teachers who were referred to earlier, and of whom forty per cent confessed themselves uneasy in maths, were probably once just those very 'bright' young children who mastered the symbol-manipulation process very quickly. Yet at the same time they were missing out on real understanding: they did not really see the point of it all, so that when they grew up they had formed the opinion that maths was more a question of sums and of the manipulation of verbal and numerical signs than of looking at the world in a special way. Even some of those teachers who are teaching modern maths seem to have this attitude.

I have done some work in preparing people for external degrees in geography at London University. Most of the students are teachers. When discussing regional geography questions (such as those introduced briefly at the beginning of this chapter) in terms of set-theory several students have commented that they never realised that modern maths had any such possible applications! We are beginning to find ourselves in a most paradoxical situation: we have computers available that can do increasingly long and complex sums far more rapidly and accurately than human beings. But the computers have to be programmed and instructed and the programming and instructing needs maths of the sort advocated in this book. Most of us will probably never need to do sums beyond the lowest personal shopping level, but increasingly large numbers of us may need to communicate with computers. We need to know more about maths and less about sums!

However, at present our young pupils are far from being able to use computers. Let us return to them and to their immediate needs. While they are learning to categorise objects and activities in complex sets, they are also learning how different objects are *ordered*. Kits can be bought from suppliers of educational toys (see the Appendix) to help in learning this. They can be useful but they are often expensive and may come to be seen by children as school-and-lesson-type objects. It is usually better to use real live objects, especially the children themselves. Ordering is essentially *comparing*: we compare one object with another to see which is longer or heavier or fatter. We may compare several objects in order to try to arrange them in some sort of order from biggest to smallest and so on. When someone is selecting a spanner to do something to his car, he usually uses a mixture of judging by eye and trial and error. Even his low level of skill is far higher than that of little children, who often seem to look at the world in very different terms from adults. Children need a lot of experience to build up even such modest repertoires.

Once more the comparing must be made pleasurable and the teacher's main function is to set up situations that will help the children notice relationships and learn the appropriate verbal symbols so that they may later describe their own experiences and understand the descriptions of others.

Within any classroom occupied by a group of children there are abundant examples and opportunities for comparing. First one can begin by comparing the children's heights. At the simplest level the children's heights can be marked and labelled appropriately on a sheet of paper pinned to the wall. Later, when the children are learning to recognize number symbols and to count, they can measure their heights against a number scale fixed to the wall. At first this scale will be crude, showing perhaps only the major divisions and half divisions (every foot and every six inches). The aim here is not to turn small children into accurate metricians, but to help them realise that we can compare lengths. 'John is three feet and a big bit, but Mary is only three feet and a little bit' is accurate enough at this stage.

Children usually find more exciting a rather different way of comparing their heights. The teacher should obtain some large sheets of coloured paper. Spread them out on the floor and let each child lie down full-length. With big pencils the other children draw round the outline of their recumbent friend and, when symbolic trousers or dress have been added to the outline, the shape can be cut out. The various shapes can be pinned to the wall in order of size and give rise to lots of conversation. The children are asked and ask each other: 'Who is biggest?', 'Who is smallest?' and so on.

This can be turned into a game. The children sit round and in turn are asked things like 'Bill, find someone who is bigger/smaller than you.' This sort of activity always seems to capture the interest of the children. They can be seen at odd times looking at the shapes, comparing them with others, and any visitor to the class is likely to be greeted with 'That's me. I'm not the smallest, am I?' or some such half-anxious, half-proud greeting.

Similar activities can be planned and carried out with weighing. Again no attempt should be made at first to use adult units of measurement. The simple relationships 'heavier than', 'lighter than' and 'as heavy as' are sufficient. Later simple units of weight can be introduced. Scales can be bought but they should be robust: the old-fashioned pan and weight type of scales are best, although they are usually too small. For comparing heavier weights (such as the children themselves) a see-saw or simple plank of wood resting on a chair is adequate.

As with the later stages of work in sets, ordering games can be used to introduce children to different forms of mathematical notation, especially graphs and other semi-pictorial methods. At the simplest level, let us say that we are comparing sizes of feet. Each child puts his foot on a piece of paper to be traced round by a friend. The shape is coloured, labelled with his name and cut out. The feet cut-outs can be arranged in order of size and stuck to a frieze around the wall. This gives a simple pictorial representation of an ordered relationship. Later, when the children are being introduced to units of measuring, the children's silhouettes can be grouped into sets: those children who are less than '3 big bits' (or feet), those between '3 and 4 big bits', and so on. Apart from the valuable language activities that arise out of this, the children are learning gradually to abstract some aspects of situations while ignoring others.

There are other sorts of ordering activities that most adults take for granted. Children have a surprisingly poorly developed sense of time. Ask a young child whether Jesus was alive when mummy was a little girl. The answer is nearly always a forthright and scornful 'No'. But then go on to ask: 'What about when granny was a little girl? Was Jesus alive then?' There is much less certainty here. Even as late as seven years some children are not sure. 'After all,' they seem to think, 'Granny is pretty old. She was a little girl a long time ago. Jesus lived a long time ago, so perhaps they were alive at the same time.' Even in some secondary schools there is a great deal of confusion about the recent and distant past. Fully developed adult time concepts are slowly built up over long periods through experience. At the earliest stages the teacher tries to introduce to her pupils the simplest ideas of time-ordering. It is not that the children do not sense the passing of time. Of course they do, but what they lack is memory and a habit of thinking that includes time as an important element. At first the teacher asks simple questions and discusses everyday sequences: we wash our hands before dinner, we have our milk before we go out to play, we go to sleep after dinner, and so on. This can lead on to little word-games that fill the odd corner of time, say after the children have washed their hands and before they go to dinner: 'What do we do before . . . ?'

Gradually the time span covered by before and after can be extended: Who came before George? Who came before grandad? Children are often intrigued to discover that there is a whole host of people who came before them stretching back into the mists of the past, and some of the more advanced even at an early age go on to ask 'Who was the *first* man? Who came before the first man?' and so on. These questions are not quaint or cute, nor should they be regarded as tiresome: they are the very roots of later scientific curiosity and the foundation of interest in history, archae-ology, geology and many other grown-up things. If the teacher knows a little about evolution then a simple answer can be given. If she doesn't then let her admit her ignorance to the children and suggest that they find out together. Sometimes children will bring fossils or pictures of 'pre-historic' animals from home. Each of these can form the starting place for a discussion that brings in ideas of 'long ago', 'before' and 'now'. It must be emphasised here that it is not history or geology that are being 'taught', but simple concepts of 'long ago', 'before' and 'after'. There are other additional benefits though: the children are listening to and using language in a natural interesting way. They are learning new vocabulary and are becoming used to the idea that conversation can be used to explore our thoughts. Beyond this there are many other advantages: they learn to take part in discussions. Sometimes they have to sit quietly and listen to other people, at other times they will be listened to. Perhaps this last point is the most important. In later school life at the secondary stage teachers often complain that their pupils are apathetic and never contribute to lessons. But very often these children have never been listened to anyway. What they say may be silly or wrong, but they deserve

courtesy: their ideas should be treated seriously and discussed on their merits. In this way errors can be eliminated
and information imparted, and the children also come to
sense that they are valued as people with valid points of view.
If this could be achieved then later education would truly
become the joint effort between teacher and student that so
many teachers hope for.

After extensive experience of working with sets and
ordering relationships children are ready to begin the more
formal work that begins to look more like maths in the usual
sense. At this stage they begin to *compare* and *match*. This is
the stage when they begin to look for correspondences
between different sets of objects and they begin to label sets
of different sizes. In many ways this can still be done
informally: for instance, children help to give out the milk.
At first they do the simple task of matching straws to bottles
and bottles to children. Very soon they come to realise that
the matching may not be perfect: there may not be enough
straws, or there may be one bottle too many and so on. At
home children can help lay the table: they learn to match a
fork with a knife and both with a spoon. Each member of the
family must be matched with a set of cutlery: extra pieces
must be put away in a drawer, or additional items sought to
make the match perfect.

More formally there are many matching exercises: cards
can be prepared with different numbers of dots or other
shapes on. Each card has a duplicate. One set of cards is laid
out and the child matches his set to the others. At first very
simple patterns are used, but later greater variation can be
introduced. At first, too, the match should be identical, as in
matching these two cards:

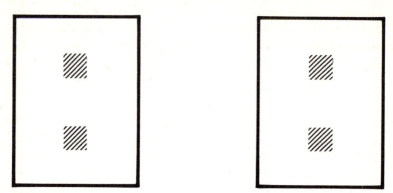

Matching exercise.   'At first the match should be identical.'

but later 'three red squares' can be matched with 'three blue squares'. It is probably best that additional problems should be introduced singly: if the colour is varied then keep the pattern similar. Later the pattern can be varied as well and still later one pattern of four motor cars can be matched with a different pattern of, say, four children. Both abstract shapes and realistic pictures cut from magazines should be used. Gradually different arrangements must be introduced. Thus 'five' may include any of these shapes:

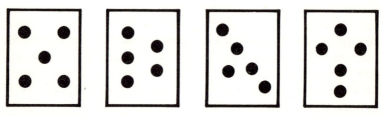

'Later the pattern can be varied. This "five" may include any of these shapes.'

In this way children do not come to associate a symbol with only one specific arrangement of dots. Cards can be bought commercially but sets can be made at home cheaply just as well. They should be stuck on tough cardboard and covered with plastic sheeting to preserve them against grubby fingers. Some form of storage in boxes and a simple cataloguing system are also useful. Cards should be neat and colourful and the aim should be to have plenty of variety so that the children practise the same sorts of perceptual and intellectual activities without getting bored.

Some children will hurry through these stages and be ready for other sorts of pre-number work, but others need much more practice. Children must not be forced to move at the pace of the quickest in the group. Nor should they move with the slowest. Ideally each child should progress at his own rate. This may be difficult to achieve in a very large class where some form of grouping may be necessary, with each child in the group being roughly at the same stage. In the rather smaller groups common in nursery classes and play-groups more individual work is usually easier to organise.

In addition to this more 'formal' work there are large numbers of games that can be used and that good teachers use to fill in the odd moments, say, when parents are arriving to take their children home, or when waiting to go into lunch. Some of these are number songs, others are more straightforward games: the children are asked to suggest how many things we have in twos: eyes, ears, feet, hands and so on. Some children can be surprisingly inventive here: two ends of a see-saw, two sisters, two gold-fish in the class aquarium and so on. Fours are relatively easy to think of: wheels and doors of cars, legs of horses and cows, members of a family, but threes are quite rare. At first the numbers should be kept small. Little children probably live in a world where anything above four is many. (Think of most adults who cannot conceive of the millions of years involved in geological time or the millions of millions of miles involved in space travel. We all have the same problems: it is just the limits of the problem that vary.)

These and similar games can be returned to over and over again. Children who may not have contributed anything during a lesson will often come up to the teacher later and confide that they have two grannies, two dogs or, on occasion, two dads. One girl once told me, quite proudly, that she had three fathers: her real one, the one her mother was married to and the one she was living with.

Gradually as confidence is gained and knowledge is built

up these games can be more formalised. The class can make a 'Number book'. Each page or set of pages is labelled

My book of three
∴ 3 ⋮

As confidence is gained and knowledge is built up these games can be more formalized and each child contributes something relevant: a picture he has drawn or cut out of a catalogue or magazine. Each picture can be labelled both with the child's name and its own name, and thus the children begin to make some acquaintance in a perfectly natural way with writing and reading. Then each child can keep his own number books, each entitled 'My book of two' (or whatever). It is better to make these books out of sugar paper with coloured cartridge paper covers, sewn together very simply, so that each book is just as large as the teacher decides is necessary: there is no point in carrying on with 'twos' when the children are ready for 'tens', merely because there are some unfilled pages in the 'twos' book.

Once the children have passed through this stage they are on the brink of more conventional maths. Let us pause a little to see just what they have been achieving. In addition to the side-benefits of conversation, boosting self-confidence and so on, at this time the children are learning to link number names with real groups of objects, both natural and artificial. By experiencing each number name linked with a large variety of different patterns of different objects they come to abstract the essential common idea. Underlying three apples, three sisters, three dogs, three circles is the common idea of *threeness*. It was mentioned earlier that to a child two flies may be more similar to three flies than to two elephants. But maths cannot be built on such impressionistic concepts. Maths can cope with the *twoness* of two and the *threeness* of three: it can do nothing with the *flyness* of flies or the *elephantness* of elephants. Therefore in order to think mathematically each child must learn to abstract the twoness from two elephants and from two flies. Because they are so used to number concepts, teachers tend to hurry their pupils along through this stage. The children can learn to give 'right' answers, but it is probably a residual memory of the sense of bafflement from this time that later handicaps most adults in their dealing with even elementary mathematical problems.

Only one major stage remains in this pre-number period: constructing the concepts of adding and subtracting — putting things together and taking them apart. By this time children will have constructed their own pre-mathematical models of the surrounding world. They will have learned during earlier water-play that by putting two small bottles of water together you can fill a larger one, or that if you spill some of your lemonade you have less to drink. Now this intuitive knowledge needs to be made more explicit. There are many commercially produced sets of apparatus that can be used at this time (see the Appendix). Essentially each scheme aims to accustom the children to the idea that if two objects are placed together one arrives at an answer which will be the same however many times the experiment is repeated. But that if you join two different objects together you will arrive at a different answer. At first the schemes depend on non-numerical activities: children put together 'a red' and 'a blue' or 'two greens' etc. In another scheme they may use 'longs' and 'flats', or coloured plastic cubes that clip together to form towers of different heights. Teachers usually help by making home-made aids. They string together wooden cotton-reels or conkers in different lengths and so on. Sometimes large coloured beads can be used and the children try to match their own sets of marbles, acorns or beads to the pattern provided by the teacher. The stimulus patterns supplied by the teacher are usually labelled with a number symbol. By matching their own productions with those of the teacher and noting the relevant symbol the children gradually link symbol with reality. At first, though, it is essentially a matching task that is being performed, together with an ordering one: if I have a 'four' and I put on another 'one' I get a 'five'.

After experience of putting things together and taking them apart again the children are introduced to more formal number work. They learn that if a 'five' and a 'two' are joined together a 'seven' results. They need lots of practice here: 'seven' results from combinations other than 'five' and 'two'. They need to experiment with lots of different combinations in order to discover that $5 + 2$, $4 + 3$, $6 + 1$ as well as $1 + 6$, $3 + 4$ and $2 + 5$ all come to the same thing. It is probably true to say that the child does not actually *know* what 'seven' or '7' *means* unless it has been linked with many different sets of seven objects, with many different 'number facts', such as those outlined above, and with the same facts expressed rather differently: that 'seven' is one more than 'six' and one less than 'eight'.

Only when these facts have been experienced practically and explored verbally has the time arrived for symbols to be used formally. Children must learn that '+' means 'and' or 'put together with', that '−' means the opposite, with one important difference that is not always made clear and that causes confusion. When we are adding it does not matter which number we take first: the answer comes out the same (with luck and skill) anyway. But the negative sign has a very different implication: we *must* start with the first number and remove the second. If we change the order we get a different answer. Finally the children must learn that '=' means 'equals', or that both 'sides' mean the same thing. Once more this is not as easy a concept to grasp as it appears. The symbol is derived from an older symbol for scales and a pair of old-fashioned scales can be usefully employed to demonstrate equality: on one side are piled the appropriate piles of bricks, say 'three' and 'five'. The scale pan is depressed until someone counts the correct number of bricks into the other pan when a balance is achieved. This point seems elementary but teachers at later stages are often surprised at the wildly inaccurate answers that are given to 'equations': it is as though the older pupils had never realised that they were trying, whenever they wrote an equation, to strike a balance. When a mistake like this is made it is usually the young person who is blamed. It would be much more just to blame the teacher of his early years who did not supply him with the appropriate experience at the right time.

Many schemes in 'modern' maths use materials that force the learners to work in different number systems. There is nothing sacred about the one we use every day. It is merely a convention. We say that it has 'a base ten', which means that we use nine different symbols (one to nine) and zero. When we fill one column we transfer to another (we 'carry a one') and begin again from one, and so on. We could equally well use a different base, say four. Then our counting would be like this: 1, 2, 3, 10 (=4), 11 (=5), etc. Adults often find this concept difficult: we are imprisoned in our own artificial mathematical concepts. Young children seem to take this sort of thing in their stride. There is no reason why they should not: one system is as natural (or unnatural) as any other. Once they have learned the importance of place value (or, conventionally, of 'tens and units') then they can very quickly learn to work with one base rather than another. Once more we see operating the fundamental psychological truth: if we really understand the concept we can learn the symbol quickly. If we concentrate on the symbol too soon then we may never master the concept.

The concept of 'zero' is probably one of the most difficult for young children to grasp. Difficulties are caused by its being used to mean both 'nothing' in everyday terms, and 'empty column' mathematically. When it occurs by itself it does not matter too much whether you think of it as nothing or as emptiness, but in combination with other symbols the difference is of the utmost importance: 0 'means' different things in 20, 200, 202, .02 etc. It is not uncommon to find children even at the secondary stage writing 'two hundred and thirty-four' as 200304. These same children can do sums 'correctly':

$$\begin{array}{r} 18 \\ + \ 16 \\ \hline 34 \end{array} \qquad \begin{array}{r} 16 \\ + \ 13 \\ \hline 29 \end{array}$$

but one wonders what '34' and '29' mean here, when 'thirty-four' is equated with '304' and 'twenty-nine' with '209'. Undoubtedly some of the children who make mistakes like these are not very clever, but the mistakes probably reflect bad teaching rather than any shortcoming in the children themselves. When these young people have reached the age of thirteen or more their state is very sad. Not only have they got to unlearn a lot of mistaken things, but they have to overcome the sense of hopelessness that years of failure and not understanding have generated. In addition they have to return to what they, their friends and parents often see as 'baby stuff'. Not unreasonably they object and reject school. They get into trouble and fall further behind, and so it goes on.

By the time the children have reached the stage we are now considering, they will have several years of valuable mathematical experience behind them. Much of this will have been gained informally. To an onlooker not much may seem to have been happening. This should not worry the teacher: she should have the courage of her professional knowledge. If one form of schooling is more useful than another then it must be used, although no opportunity of educating parents and laymen should be lost. Parents have a right to know and most of them are keenly interested in knowing what their children are doing.

Later there will be need for much learning by heart. If one is 'doing a sum' like adding a column of figures

$$\begin{array}{r} 18 \\ 27 \\ 34 \\ + \ 16 \end{array}$$

it saves time when we are adding these figures, actually to *know* that 'eight and seven are fifteen — and four, nineteen — and six, twenty-five,' and so on. These basic number facts can be learned only by lots of practice, especially practice under conditions of speed (the rapid-fire 'mental arithmetic' of older days). But this practice should come later, after lengthy experience with more fundamental mathematical thinking. With this essential preliminary experience the rote-learning will come easily enough. Without it, it will probably be delayed and *may never come*. The author has observed student teachers in colleges of education counting on their fingers or adding the tell-tale counting marks beside a column of figures.

$$
\begin{array}{r}
18 \\
27 \;\vdots\!\vdots. \\
34 \;\vdots\;\vdots \\
+\;16 \;\vdots\;\vdots \\
\hline
95
\end{array}
$$

Many young children do this. I did it myself until I became a pay clerk in the army and sheer lack of time forced me into a more efficient method of computation.

For many teachers and psychologists 'rote-learning' and 'formal work' are dirty words. This attitude is nonsense. Rote-learning has a part, and an important part, to play in intellectual development. It helps to speed up the more mechanical aspects of intellectual functioning and this releases the person for more useful activities. If we exhaust ourselves doing simple counting and addition we may lose sight of the real meaning of the activity. Rote-learning of the number bonds (that is, instant recognition of the sums of different digits) prevents us from wasting time on trivialities. But rote-learning must not replace meaningful experience. Rich experience must come first. Out of it the basic concepts will begin to grow. When these concepts are well rooted and flourishing then is the time to introduce some rote-learning. Rote-learning is a means to an end. All too often it has become an end in itself and the real end of education has been lost sight of.

6 Social and emotional growth

In introductory texts on psychology it is traditional to discuss emotional growth, personality, social development and intellectual growth in different chapters. We find some psychologists who claim to be specialists in 'personality' and others in 'cognition'. Each of these specialists has a very different approach to his interest, and each often scorns the practitioners in another field. In part this 'closed-shop' tendency stems from the academic need for researchers to specialise in one field or another since few people can keep up to date in many very different areas. In part, too, it derives from different approaches to human problems: emotional and personality problems are largely the concern of the clinical psychologist, the psychiatrist and the child guidance worker. These people are faced with the urgent tasks of helping their patients *now*. They cannot spend the many years in research necessary to sort out all the theoretical and practical problems that intrigue the professional researcher in cognition who may spend his whole working life investigating the way in which young children form, let us say, mathematical or linguistic concepts.

There is a third major reason for the differences: some people feel that human nature is unique and complex, that one somehow lessens the stature of man by studying him statistically and scientifically, that one should use one's flair and intuition when coping with humans in urgent and desperate need. The more scientific workers on the other hand point out that medicine only made progress when doctors began to study their patients scientifically. They argue that only when psychology grows out of its 'pre-scientific' phase, however much this may pain the romantics among us, will we really begin to understand man and be in a position to help him as he needs. They also point out that intuition and flair often appear to fail, especially when an independent investigator who does not share the assumption of the clinician tries to discover whether, say, the patient is any better for his treatment, or whether he may even have been made worse.

Let us forget about this academic squabbling for the moment and try to discover what the various different 'schools' of psychology can tell us about social and emotional growth. All the many and diverse approaches to psychology can be grouped into three major schools: the behaviourists, the psychoanalysts and the third, who do not seem to have acquired a name yet.

Briefly, the *behaviourists* see our personality as the sum total of all our past reinforcement schedules. By this they mean that if, in the past, we have done something and been reinforced (or rewarded) for it, then we are likely to do it again in the future. The reward need not be something tangible, although parents do often give their children a real, physical reward such as a bicycle for passing an examination or money or sweets for doing something they approve of. Every parent or teacher who punishes a child, whether by smacking, sending to bed early or keeping in at playtime, is trying to use a crude form of conditioning. They hope that the behaviour that is being linked with punishment will tend not to occur again. It is not very effective for most children, but the adults still keep on. One wonders why until we realise that for humans reinforcement need not be physical: it may be social or emotional. A word of praise from someone we admire, a feeling of pleasure, or a sense of power (perhaps just of being 'boss' now and again) are all reinforcing. To punish someone gives a sense of power to the punisher. That is why it is so popular and universal.

Examples have been given elsewhere of reinforcement in everyday situations. Other examples are not difficult to find. Young women, for example, are very good reinforcers of young men they have decided will make suitable potential husbands. They listen attentively and sometimes participate in wet and muddy sports like sailing or supporting the local rugby club, or they make appropriate noises expressing interest in dull and boring topics such as politics, motor cars or philosophy. The attention, the appropriate girlish noises and the sparkling look of interest all boost the male ego of the young man marked down for sacrifice. Young men like, among other things, their egos to be boosted so this keeps them talking to the cunning female amateur psychologist and, more importantly from her point of view, keeps them away from the other cunning female amateur psychologists. Exclusive male attention appears to be reinforcing to young women and this maintains the necessary behaviour patterns in the women. As with the woman psychologist and her baby a mutually reinforcing pair-situation is operating. In this case it frequently achieves the desired union. Thereafter the reciprocal reinforcement, alas, often seems to diminish.

In Chapter 2 it was shown why punishment often does not seem to work: the effects of the punishment may be counteracted by reinforcement from other sources. Another powerful reason was also discussed: punishment can block a wrong turning but it does not point out the correct one. Let us imagine that a little child can do any one of twenty possible things in a given situation, only one of which is correct (that is, desired by his parents or teachers). He chooses a wrong one. He is punished and may never do that thing again, but *he still has eighteen possible mistakes to make*. If he makes several wrong turnings and on each occasion is punished, reprimanded or ridiculed, then the parent or teacher may become counter-reinforcing in himself: when the child finally hits on the right way, no amount of praise from the adult will have any effect. The child has just 'switched off'. Of course most teachers and parents link advice and instruction with the punishment. If this is done in terms that the child can understand and if the child is not too resentful at whatever punishment or reprimand he has received, it might have some effect. It would be better to arrange a situation in which the child cannot help making the right choice and then reinforce him: a word of thanks or the comment that it was a 'grown-up' thing to do, perhaps a smile and a ruffling of the hair, are often all that are needed.

The lesson in this for teachers and parents is simple: whenever some behaviour that you want occurs, then reinforce it. It will probably occur again and again. At first reinforcement is needed on each occasion, but once the behaviour has become frequent then it is more powerful to reinforce it at irregular and widely spaced out intervals. All this sounds very much like brain-washing. It seems too calculated for many people and none of us likes someone who appears to be manipulating us. Reinforcing people *can* be manipulative, yet, if we want our children to grow up thoughtful of others, unselfish, polite and tolerant, we must encourage this when they are young. If you do not like the word reinforcement, then call it encouragement. Whatever we call it, we all practise it at some time or other. We send children to school to be manipulated intellectually: we approve of the teacher who is good at getting her pupils to read, to learn maths and to do neat craftwork. It is only in the areas of personality that we feel that children should be totally free. Of course they are not free at all: if *we* do not encourage one form of behaviour, *others* will encourage another, often one that we do not wish or like. Children do not live in a completely independent little world. They interact with others, and once this interaction takes place, then reinforcement of one sort or another begins.

Behaviourists, then, see personality developing, as it were, from the outside: we are what we have been made. A rather older model of personality development and one that has been very influential in clinical psychiatry and much of the literature on the development of early childhood is the *psychoanalytical*. This was initiated by Sigmund Freud, a Viennese neurologist, but it has since been extended by many later workers. In general it sees each individual as a bundle of dynamic forces, which are channelled now one way, now another, depending on all sorts of natural and artificial blocks. Freud believed that at birth we are endowed with a very primitive set of selfish aggressive and sensuous drives. Together these constitute the *id* and are inherited from distant, primitive ancestors. As we grow these primitive Id drives are socialised: we gradually learn to control them consciously (although the controlling mechanism itself is largely unconscious) and thus we construct our *egos*. At the same time we are learning and absorbing the social and personal values of our parents. This learning is responsible for the growth of the moral side of our personality: our *superegos*. Although the ego and superego are very much influenced by society and learning, the real force in our personality dynamics is seen as the supply of primitive psychic force, or *libido*, that is utilised in fuelling ego functions (thinking, learning, remembering), in maintaining our moral values (superego functions), or it may break out in uncontrolled rage and sexual activity, when we are dominated by our ids. It is believed, too, that if this libido is not allowed to appear in one place it will, like the flood waters of a raging torrent, appear elsewhere, often doing a lot of damage on the way.

Although there is absolutely no evidence for the existence of any of these forces and drives, and there is in fact considerable evidence that they do not exist, the dynamic model of personality, as it is called, has had great influence in the modern world, especially the idea of repressing the libido. If damming up a torrent is dangerous, so will be the damming up or blocking off of powerful psychic forces. This blocking or repressing, it is felt, may cause the psychic force to be frustrated and to burst out in destructive antisocial behaviour, or it may be turned inwards on the person himself, causing neuroses and psychosomatic illnesses or, in the extreme, suicide. It is this (largely mistaken) belief in the evils of repression that has led to the emphasising of extreme freedom in education. We must not, it is argued, repress any natural instinct. If we do then we might damage the emotional development of the individual for life. Since creativity was also linked with the free play of the libido it was felt that if we could allow the libido total freedom we would help our young pupils to be more creative.

Apart from the lack of any scientifically acceptable supporting evidence for the truth of these statements, there is much evidence that they are invalid. Mere observation alone suggests that most creative artists are not, in their art at least, totally free: musicians submit themselves to a rigorous training in harmony, counterpoint and orchestration, artists learn technique often over many years, and so on. Before most creative scientists can do any useful original, creative work they must undergo training and study lasting, perhaps, for the first thirty years of their lives.

Whatever the theoretical and practical shortcomings of this model, it is clear that it sees our personalities as largely developing from within, as opposed to the behavioural model which sees them as developing in response to outside forces. In both cases the individual seems to have very little actual control over what he is and what he does.

There is a third model that has developed more recently in psychology. In general it has not been applied to personality and clinical studies to the same extent as to intellectual development. Briefly, according to this model, we can see the same forces at work in personality development as we can in other areas of psychology: given different experiences, the child tries to make sense of them. If he sees around him people who are courteous and gentle (without being hypocritical and dishonest) then he is likely to construct for himself a social model in which people, including himself, are responsible, thoughtful, courteous and kind. On the other hand, if the important people in his life spend much of their time in dishonest pursuits, hitting their wives over the head with bottles and so on, then this is likely to be what the child comes to accept as normal behaviour. Of course the process is not simply mechanical and inevitable. The growing child may gradually construct a model of society and personality that is very divergent from that of his family. In part this is a result of the fact that each of us is exposed to many different models from relatives, friends, teachers and others. We have to evaluate them and incorporate them into our own world pictures. In part, too, it may be because children do not see the world in the same terms as their parents. The husband may see his wife as a nagging shrew who makes him feel uncomfortable when he comes home full of beer and bonhomie and who deserves a clip round the ear to make her shut up. To his son she may be someone who provides love and warmth. How he will react in adult life to his wife will depend, other things being equal, partly on whether he sees her in similar terms to his mother, partly on how his circle of acquaintances views the husband—wife situation and partly on how his wife behaves.

Because children do not often talk to adults about what

concerns them most, it would be a mistake to imagine that they do not care. Once, when I was teaching in a boarding school for handicapped children, an eleven-year-old boy approached me with what was clearly a very important question:

'When you're married, sir, does your wife always hit you over the head with a bottle?'

'No, Henry, why?'

'Well, my mam does to my dad.'

This boy was rather older than the children discussed in this book, but the example given earlier of small children trying to understand how a teacher can, in turn, have a teacher, is part of the same process of trying to understand the world.

Children are great observers. In fact, they probably observe more accurately than they understand verbal explanations. This appears to underlie the fact that in so many fields children do what they see their parents and teachers doing rather than heed what they are saying. It is no use our telling our children to halt at the kerb and look left and right, if we have the habit of dashing across the road without waiting. Nor does it make sense to a child to be told always to use a zebra crossing when mum and dad cannot be bothered to walk twenty yards or so to use one. Parents often justify their behaviour by claiming to be in a hurry. But children are also often in a hurry and have less ability to judge whether it is safe to cross a busy road or not.

Let us see whether we can apply these rather general considerations to nursery classes and playgroups. The key facts to remember are:

children observe what is going on round them;

they try to make sense of what they see, and build for themselves models of social behaviour, on the basis of their observations;

they use these models to guide their own behaviour.

The models that children construct are often faulty: the children may not have much opportunity to observe a very large sample of behaviour and their intellectual skills may not be fully developed. In addition they may have been exposed to conflicting models at home or at play. Teachers must accept the fact that there are limits to their influence.

Within these limits, however, teachers can do very much. It is not uncommon to hear older children talking in tones of considerable awe about the teachers in their infant class. My children, even in late adolescence, straightened themselves up and smoothed hair and dresses if they saw their former infants' mistress approaching. Teachers must consider what sort of behaviour they desire. Thereafter they must set up situations that will encourage this behaviour. If they want their pupils to be tolerant, helpful and fair, then the children must see around them adults who are tolerant, helpful and fair. This is not always as easy as it seems. Adults sometimes feel under the weather or get tired. Youthful waywardness can be very trying towards the end of a long term on a wet Friday afternoon. Sometimes we teachers show our annoyance or tiredness. This is not necessarily a bad thing: children have to live in a real world, and teachers are not angels. What is surprising is that when one adult snaps at another it is not uncommon for him to apologise later, yet many teachers would never dream of apologising to a child. On the other hand they often insist that children apologise to each other after some quarrel or upset. This seems to be a very questionable habit: children will do what we do, not what we say. At least, they will do what we say, but they will not mean it: we teach them to be hypocrites and eventually to despise adults, especially their teachers.

Another reason for apparent childish lapses from desired behaviour is that children often *are* selfish, in the sense that for them the self is the centre of the universe. The adult may want a child to share his toy with another child: cooperation is always desirable. Yet the child may not want to share his toy, he may on the contrary want it for himself. This is not necessarily evidence of total moral depravity. After all most adults would not willingly share their cars with anyone who feels he has a right to ask for them. We would almost certainly call the police if someone insisted on 'borrowing' our car in spite of our wishes! We should be at least as tolerant of childish selfishness as we are of our own.

Sensitivity is needed in situations like these. If the child is adamant about not sharing, our insistence will probably achieve nothing except tantrums and tears. When it is all over we shall have the new problem of smoothing ruffled feelings, while the second child may well have lost interest in the once-desired object. Anyway in such a situation it is probably better to try to distract the second child's attention towards some other attractive toy or activity. Such advice should not be taken to imply that we must give up all attempts to achieve sharing or any other behaviour we desire. It may mean that we have to work a little harder and more subtly.

It is in cases like these that we can use techniques of behaviour modification: if we want children to share then on any occasion when they do so we must reinforce their behaviour with a smile or word of praise. Reinforced behaviour is likely to occur anew on later occasions. Gradually, by this means, we construct an environment in which many children are cooperative, helpful and sharing — not all the time, but quite frequently. As a result any new child coming into our class will be experiencing an environment in which other desired behaviour can operate: children learn very quickly whether it is safe to experiment, or whether they will be reprimanded if they make a mess, whether they will be laughed at if they offer suggestions, or whether their contributions will be accepted and treated courteously, whether unselfish and thoughtful behaviour, care for the younger children and animals, washing hands before meals, not destroying the toys of others, are the norm or so unusual as to excite comment.

Probably no single specific activity will achieve any of these: it is the whole style of the class or group that is important. This is why it is often easier to maintain a happy, calm, busy atmosphere in a group that has been in operation for some time than in one newly formed. But in the latter case much can be achieved by having plenty of exciting, interesting activities available, by setting up situations where children can play together or separately, by intervening at the right moment to avert catastrophe or prevent murder, and above all by being calm: a quiet word of praise achieves much more than a steady stream of reprimands or constant nagging.

This last point is especially important. There is a lot of evidence that children imitate the example of people who are important to them. It has been demonstrated that children who are shown films of their teachers or an older child beating and kicking a doll tend to do the same. It is important to realise the full significance of this research. It has sometimes been interpreted as evidence in favour of the alleged evils of violence on film and television, although it is questionable whether this is valid. Little children seem to copy people they admire and know: parents, teachers and older children, that is, ordinary people. There is no evidence that the violence of a Tom and Jerry cartoon or a cowboy film has any effect on the behaviour of children, who are often more sophisticated than many adults imagine. Questioning them reveals very quickly that they distinguish clearly between reality and the unreality of much of what they see on the screen. Much greater contributions to general aggressiveness probably derive from other circumstances: almost all children are exposed to ordinary adults being aggressive: mum and dad quarrel, dad drives aggressively and swears at other motorists, the teacher loses her temper. These are *real* people, wearing ordinary clothes in everyday situations who are being emotional. A child is more likely to copy them than someone speaking in a strange accent and wearing an exotic costume, waving a revolver and riding a horse. It is probably young adults who are influenced more by ritualised aggression on films and television than little children, yet no one has suggested excluding young men from cinemas.

Yet on the other hand real life is full of frustrations: the toy we wanted to play with is already in use, the colours we wanted to paint with have just been spilled, Mary won't move away and let me roll my car up and down the floor. Just as with adults, children often react to frustration with aggression. Part of the job of teachers is to teach their children to tolerate at least some amounts of frustration: nothing is more comic than the choleric retired army colonel who loses his temper and shouts at the slightest of hitches. We do not want our children to behave like this. This means that the teacher may have to step in and offer distractions and explanations. Later a story can be used to point a moral when everyone has calmed down and ruffled feelings are soothed.

Stories are of immense use with children of all ages. At this stage the stories are best kept simple, with only a few characters. The heroes and heroines are usually shown doing brave or thoughtful acts and reaping their just reward: the naughty animals or children often come to a sticky end, suitably softened for the sake of humanity. Stories should not be undervalued. As we shall see later, stories play an important part in the language and pre-reading development of children. They are useful too in developing and strengthening the general atmosphere that the teacher is trying to create in her class or nursery group. They also provide a very useful focal point around which the nursery day revolves. Many expert teachers use their story periods as 'settling down sessions': the children have worked and played busily all the morning. They help to tidy up, and wash their hands for lunch or before going home. Then comes the quiet period when children settle down on rugs and mats in the 'book corner' to listen to a story. Some stories can be told, others read (perhaps changing any inappropriate language). It is useful for the teacher always to have a book on her lap when telling a story: illustrations can be used to help the less imaginative to follow, and, as will be seen later, it is important to associate books with pleasant activities, so that the books themselves will come to be seen as pleasant.

It may be queried why I link together emotional and social development: they are often treated as separate considerations. Apart from the dangers of fragmenting descriptions of human beings, there are other more important reasons for looking at them together. In the first place it must not be thought that people are extremely emotional or self-controlled in isolation from their cultural and social surroundings. It may be, for example and as many Britons believe, that all or most Italians are noisy, gregarious, emotional and music-loving. Personally, I am sceptical: I have met many Italians who are not like this at all. But let us, for the moment, assume it is correct. Now the question arises: is there a genetic, inborn reason for this set of behaviour patterns? Do other nations who (it is widely believed) exhibit very different personal and social traits have different sets of genes in their make-up? This is extremely unlikely. What is more probable is that each different culture reinforces different kinds of behaviour in its young. If English secondary school children tend to sit in rows in a classroom, making notes and not speaking much, this is because the English as a whole and teachers in particular tend to value and expect this kind of behaviour in children of secondary school age. Children who behave as expected are rewarded, or at least are not punished, while those who do the unexpected may incur the teacher's displeasure. I have heard more than one secondary teacher, talking of the new annual intake of children from primary schools, say 'We'll have to knock the habit of interrupting lessons and making comments out of this lot.' Many primary teachers value the contributions that their pupils make and encourage them with praise and other reinforcements. As a result the desired behaviour increases in frequency, but teachers of older children who see education in a very different light seek to extinguish the unwanted behaviour and to establish new patterns. Children are usually very malleable and the teachers have their reward *in the short run*. It is unfortunate that later, when their pupils are fourteen or fifteen years old, the teachers may complain of apathy, by which they mean, among other things, an unwillingness to make contributions to lessons and a lack of commitment to education. But it is not surprising: this is exactly the kind of behaviour that they have wittingly or unwittingly reinforced in the preceding years.

An additional reason for linking emotional and social behaviour as socially valuable or as maladjusted is because we cannot judge behaviour except in terms of the society we live in. This is clearly seen in the perennial conflict between educational psychologists and many teachers: the latter tend to see maladjustment in terms of bad behaviour, while the former see the excessive 'goodness' (reflected in sitting quietly, in withdrawing from normal noisy school life and in a total lack of rebelliousness) as being more serious. Neither is wrong: each has a different point of view. The teacher has the problem of trying to get thirty or forty noisy and often wayward and thoughtless children down to the hard task of learning something. Under these circumstances the 'good' child is a welcome bonus and the awkward one a nuisance. The psychologists see a certain amount of self-assertiveness as essential for full development, but they tend to deal with only one customer at a time and are thus able to tolerate more disruption.

Teachers in any one school often disagree among themselves as to the correct evaluation of any individual child: some teachers see a wisecracking interrupter of lessons as potentially creative and a person who provides light relief. Other teachers may see him as a ruddy menace who needs slapping down. Such differences must be accepted: there is no one single right view of personality. Personality is seen from the standpoint of what is expected and accepted as normal. It is only when parents, teachers and the members of the child's own group of friends and associates concur in seeing behaviour as unacceptable that urgent attention is needed. The individual probably is *maladjusted*, in the sense that he does not fit into his bit of society anywhere. Special educational treatment may be needed, and this usually involves a two-sided attack on the problem: on the one hand helping the child to withstand the many multiple and often conflicting demands that are made on him by different people and, on the other, trying to modify his behaviour so that it becomes acceptable to the people around.

Many teachers are faced with 'problem' children. The problems these children pose are usually those of unacceptable behaviour: excessive weeping and clinging, bullying, destructiveness, use of violent behaviour and bad language. Many of these children — the so-called 'maladjusted' children — are under treatment at the child guidance clinic (or waiting for it). It must be remembered that *maladjustment* is not a disease like measles or appendicitis. It merely indicates that the child does not fit into his society. This may have several different causes: the children may be too bright or too dull. His home may be violent. The home may be breaking up and the child's security destroyed. On at least one occasion when I was working in a child guidance clinic, I became convinced that the cause of severe maladjustment in several children was their *teacher*.

The work of the psychologist is to diagnose the cause of the maladjustment and to help the teacher to set up situations which will enable the child to construct more adaptive social models on which to base his behaviour.

The essential point as regards the children that readers of this book are likely to be considered with is that it takes anyone, child or adult, time to sum up any situation and to settle down. New entrants to nursery classes or playgroups may be expected to be upset. They may need to cuddle up to a teacher or a beloved doll or teddy-bear for comfort and security. Gradually they regain confidence and begin to explore their new environment, making friends and finding new interests. Initial clinging behaviour must be accepted, but discreetly: if too much fuss is made by the teacher this may come to be reinforcing and the period of the child's initial insecurity may be unintentionally lengthened. This earlier insecurity and unhappiness is often increased by the fact that for the first time in his short life the young child is moving out of the small circle of his home, where he has a secure routine and is a very important person, into a much larger circle with a new routine and where he is only one of many. In addition, especially if he is the first child in a family, his mother may be apprehensive about what is going to happen to him. In this case it is very easy for the mother's fears and worries to be transmitted to the child.

Great care is needed on the part of the teacher or playgroup leader in the early days when new children are coming to school for the first time. If there are several new children then it is often useful to 'stagger' the induction: a few new children to come each day. Their mothers can talk at length with the teachers and look at the facilities and activities that are going on, while the children gain confidence by seeing their mothers in the classroom and are less likely to be upset by lots of other children who, equally new and insecure, may be crying. It is often useful, too, to encourage mothers of new children to spend, for a week or so, part of every morning in the class, sitting down quietly in a corner, talking to the teacher or her helpers. In this way the child can keep an eye on his mother and thus gain reassurance that the whole world has not suddenly changed. Most nursery classes and play groups also encourage mothers to bring their children to visit the school for one or two visits some time before the official entry date, so that they can sample the delights of the new experience. Mothers can then prepare their children by talking about the other boys and girls, the toys, stories and all the other delights in store for their children.

So far emotional and social development have been discussed in terms of enabling a child to take his place with confidence and security in a new group. This is of the utmost importance since as he grows older the child will have to become used to moving from one group to another. Self-confidence is gradually acquired through accepting and being accepted by other people, and this is best achieved by setting up situations in which fair play, stability, calmness and security reign. This is the essential background against which children can acquire social and emotional competence through their play experiences. But against this background there are many other determinants of playing. It is possible to ascribe these to several different causes, but it is most useful to see them as further attempts by the child to make sense of and thus understand his experiences.

Much play has been described in terms of allowing free rein to fantasy. Certainly children do appear to call into play a great deal of imagination often of the wildest sort. Their fantasy play seems to have two main lines of expression. On the one hand a few dressing-up clothes and stage props form the basis for play as firemen, policemen, soldiers, cowboys, or whatever. It is essential for every nursery class to have one or more dressing-up boxes. These can contain old clothes: shawls, bridal head-dresses, pairs of discarded high-heeled shoes, handbags, wellington boots, lengths of cloth (old curtains, bedspreads and tablecloths will do) and so on. Pieces of rope, a few carts, several large boxes, planks of wood, old lengths of hosepipe are useful, and the rest can safely be left to the children.

Children observe many different adult occupations, some of which fascinate them, but few of which they really understand. By playing at being a doctor or postman it is probable that they are trying, by experiment, to find out what it is like to be an adult. If we watch the fantasy play of children observantly we can often gain valuable insight into their current worries and obsessions as well as into some of their family relationships. The little boy, carrying an old black bag and with a toy stethoscope around his neck, who reprimands a friend 'You mustn't be rude to a doctor', certainly has observed something of value about the social position of doctors in contemporary life. It is probably also pleasant to be in a position where one's friends must not be rude to you: little children are often very rude to each other.

It is also probably safe to bet that the little girl who, dressed as a nurse, administers 'pretended' injections to all her friends with a blunt pencil, has recently been to hospital or been seen by the district nurse. Little children do not understand why they should be hurt by doctors and nurses, even though their parents try to reassure them about injections. By returning to the experience over and over again in play children seem to be trying to come to terms with their fears. There may also be some infantile malice in making one's friends submit to probably painful injections. Children are human too!

This desire to understand or come to terms with some frightening experience by returning to it in a play situation may also lie at the root of the fascination with playing at ghosts or monsters, wearing sheets or masks, that sometimes sweeps through schools. It is as though being frightened by a ghost (who is really Jimmy Smith) in a secure setting is rather delicious. It may also provide some practice through habituation under conditions of minimal danger in coming to accept some of the more baffling and incomprehensible aspects of everyday life.

We see then that the main contribution that play can make to emotional and social development is in allowing each child to experience a number of social and personal situations within a generally stable, fair and humane setting. At times the child will be able to share the toys and activities of the other children, and will come to expect them to share his toys and activities. At other times he will be able to play alone. At an early stage children often play alongside each other without much interaction. Later real cooperative play will develop. The younger child will be able to imitate the older children, teachers and helpers who behave quietly and tolerantly, who show concern for others and who can be relied on for sympathy and help in difficulty. These older people will also on occasion make him 'feel good'.

Through lengthy experience of these sorts of social interactions, the children will form for themselves a picture of society and social intercourse, with their position in it. Much of our self-opinion depends on the opinions that other important people have of us. If we are seen as worthwhile, if we are listened to courteously when we speak, if we have personal rights and if responsibilities (that are well within our competence) are laid on us, then we will come in turn to see ourselves as worthwhile, courteous and responsible.

In order to achieve this, especially when there are many children around, a great deal of space is needed. This is usually available in nursery schools and infant schools, but may be more difficult to find in a less formally organised playgroup. Some advice on this problem, together with some hints on the best way to arrange the many necessary varied activity areas and play spaces will be given later, in Chapter 9.

7 Language development and getting ready for reading

One of the most important skills that man can acquire is the ability to read. Without this ability he is thrown back on learning only what he has himself observed and experienced, or what he can hear others talk about. When most people cannot read, each generation has to rediscover many useful things for itself over and over again; but if we can read we have accessible to us all that has been done, discovered and thought by men and women of other ages and other lands. Today, once a scientist has discovered some new valuable technique or product and has published his results in a technical journal, other scientists all over the world can take up his ideas, test them in different ways and extend them. Without the ability to communicate by reading and writing, each discovery would remain the personal property of a very restricted set of people who were in the habit of meeting and talking to each other.

Of course one can go through much of life without reading anything: for most of us our entertainment is provided by radio or television and the same media supply us with the most up-to-date information about wars, catastrophes and so on. In fact, though, most people do read something and it is a mistake to imagine that only the best literature is worthwhile. In any case most of us sometimes read rubbish.

It may be that in any class of young children the majority will not read much in adult life, and some teachers have been heard to wonder why so much time and money are spent in teaching reading to so many people with so small a tangible result. Such thinking often leads on to suggestions that perhaps we should spend less time trying to teach this largely unused skill. I believe such a view to be very wrong: we cannot know in advance which of our pupils will be readers and which not. Each must be given the opportunity to learn.

In addition, as leisure time increases with technological advances in automation, more people will want to fill in some at least of their empty hours with reading. These beliefs should not be taken to imply that the author is satisfied with the present state and results of the teaching or reading. It is probable that it could be done more efficiently, in much less time and with fewer failures. It is quite possible that the majority of our reading failures are actually made that way by wrong teaching methods applied at the wrong times.

It must be emphasised that the children whose needs are discussed in this book should not be taught reading. The suggestions given later in this chapter should be seen as more appropriately *preparation for reading*. Of course some children only three or four years old will be ready to begin and some may already have begun to read. The great philosopher John Stuart Mill is reputed to have read Gibbon's *Decline and Fall of the Roman Empire* at the age of two. Most of our children are not as advanced as that. None the less some very young children may be ready to start trying to read, and in any nursery class or playgroup it is as well to have a few simple beginner's books for them to play about with. It is probably better, however, to put off any formal introduction to reading until a rather later stage: to delay a year or even longer is probably not too serious and will, in any case, soon be made up when the real work begins. Some delay will probably also make the subsequent learning more pleasant.

What is meant by the term 'reading readiness'? How can we tell whether a child is ready to begin reading or not? In outline the answer is simple: when a child shows himself trying to work things out for himself. My son, aged four, one day pointed to a bus stop sign and said: 'That's a *sssss*, isn't it?' When asked how he knew, he replied, 'Because it ends 'bus' and begins 'stop'. He had grown up in an excessively talkative family, almost innundated with books. Reading was clearly important and he was beginning to work things out for himself. He had asked earlier what the words 'said' on the bus stop sign. In fact he did not begin to learn to read formally until he started school, and seemed hardly to read at all until he discovered science fiction in early adolescence.

This delay does not seem to have had any bad effects on his subsequent development.

Unfortunately many children do not seem to reach this stage of readiness for formal reading, especially if they grow up in homes where books are not common. But if the child cannot show us that he is ready for reading, how are we to find out? This is probably one of the most critical questions that face the teacher of young children. It is frequently assumed that reaching the age of six is enough. For most children it probably is, but we need much more accurate information if we are to avoid the dangers of too early an introduction to reading. As with other cognitive skills, if a child is introduced to formal work before he is really ready for it he is not going to learn very readily. Even worse is that a sense of failure, repeated over many years, may gradually build up in the child a very powerful barrier against reading. Every survey of the reading abilities of school-leavers shows that about twenty per cent of young people are illiterate at the age of sixteen. A large proportion of these have very likely been made to fail by being taught to read too early. 'Reading readiness' is not something in itself; it is something the teacher *creates*. One of America's foremost psychologists writes: 'The idea of readiness is a mischievous half-truth. It is a half-truth because it turns out that one *teaches* readiness or provides opportunities for its nurture, one does not simply wait for it. Readiness, in these terms, consists of mastery of those simpler skills that permit one to reach higher skills.' (Jerome Bruner, *Toward a Theory of Institution*.)

This still leaves the questions of how we are to assess reading readiness. What does it consist of? It is easy to describe the state in general terms, but much less easy to be specific. This is because it is only recently that we have begun to sort out the various skills that are actually used in reading. Most of the standard books on teaching reading are, in fact of very little value. They are usually descriptions of the method used by a successful teacher written without any great knowledge of either psychology or linguistics. Of course, many of the children who were subjected to one method or another *did* learn to read, so the reader may rightly be suspicious of the author's rather cavalier statement.

However, it is probable that the children learned to read in the same way that they learned to talk: by being exposed to a lot of reading matter in the one case, to a lot of speech in the other. It is a fact that we do not know how children acquire their mother tongue, although we do know that they must be exposed to it. Those children who hear a lot of good, fluent and accurate conversation, whose parents talk and read to them, in turn grow up to use good, fluent and accurate language. Those children who do not have this advantage often grow up handicapped in many ways. It is fortunate that we do not know much about how to teach language: if we did we would undoubtedly try to 'teach' this skill and we would probably end up with about twenty per cent of our school leavers unable to open their mouths.

Recent research is beginning to demonstrate the skills that we use in reading, and once we really understand them we may be in a position to set up optimal situations to help children to acquire them for themselves. Fortunately a very good introductory account of recent work is available. This is *Understanding Reading* by Frank Smith, and is published by Holt, Rinehart and Winston. It has been praised by experienced teachers and qualified psychologists alike, and it cannot be too warmly recommended to anyone seriously concerned with the problem. The lessons from this recent research can be grouped into three main principles:

1   Whatever the teacher does, it is the child who must actually do the learning. He needs motivation and experience, and it is especially these that teachers can and should provide.

2   From this experience the child tries to abstract rules that will guide him in his use of language and reading. Examples can be found fairly commonly of this attempt to 'make sense' of data. I remember clearly (when I was seven years old) meeting in a book the word 'an', in a situation where 'and' would have been expected. I worked out a set of rules to cover this apparently anomalous usage and used it consistently until the age of thirteen, when threat of punishment and increasing evidence of counter-examples caused me to abandon my earlier hypothesis. Another example is the case of an adolescent who frequently used the

words 'you was'. He was, in true schoolmasterly fashion, reprimanded for it, until one day it was noticed that he also, on occasion, used 'you were'. When asked why sometimes he used one and sometimes the other he replied simply, 'When it's singular you use "you was", when it's plural you use "you were".' He was clearly working on the analogy of 'I was' and 'we were', probably on the basis of having heard both forms by adults. It is probable that many other childish errors represent the same attempt on the part of the children to construct their own rules. Certainly research shows that *all* children do this. Their rules are often wrong: sometimes the experience they have is faulty (it was probably a misprint in the case of the 'an/and' confusion), sometimes they have not acquired the skills to formulate really accurate rules.

3   When we listen to someone talking or when we read something, we contribute as much to the message as we get from the inside. *Our brains are as important in reading and listening as our eyes and ears.* It is clear that if we do not know Russian, for example, we cannot read it. We may begin to learn some of the language but we still stumble over some passages, even when we know all the words and the grammatical forms that are being used. As our knowledge of vocabulary and grammar and our experience increase then we read more and more rapidly until we may be able to read, say, a newspaper as easily as we would an English newspaper, skimming over the articles rapidly but extracting most of the information contained therein. In this late stage we are using lots more knowledge of Russian than is actually contained in the passage we are reading. We use, for example, our knowledge of what words are likely to occur, of the social and literary implications of various statements, and so on. Let me give examples:

(a) Very few of the readers would be able to complete the following utterance:

'Rabochy vsyekh stran s . . . ';

(b) on the other hand the majority, if they are English, should have no difficulty in finishing off:

'The boy stood on the burning d . . . ' or
'Our father which art in h . . . ' while

(c) most would assume that the following sentence contained a misprint:

'Mary married her friend's widow.'

Readers cannot complete the sentence in (a) because they do not know Russian, but (b) and (c) are easy because they know a lot of English. In part this is due to sheer learning of phrases, but it goes well beyond that. You must take my word for it that (a) should end 'soyedinyaetyes', but if I completed (b) with 'drink', you would know it was wrong, even if you were totally unacquainted with the celebrated poem. You know that one cannot stand on drink. Knowledge of wartime air force slang might suggest that you could stand in it, if the sea were covered with burning oil, but then 'on' would clearly be a mistake. Similarly, in (c) if Mary actually did the marrying then it must have been a 'widower' she wed. If the spouse were indeed a widow, then it could not be Mary who was involved, but some man, in which case 'her' is also wrong. It may appear tedious to spell out these rather trivial examples at such length, but the points that are being made are of the greatest importance: when we know a language we do not just know words and grammar. We also know the probabilities with which words come together, and we use this knowledge continuously to help us understand. Experiments have shown that it is possible to distort a telephone message by as much as sixty per cent without impairing understanding: the listener merely complains about a bad line. He does not realise that he is in fact adding more to it than he is getting from the message itself! This is how we actually read a passage in a book. We do it quickly because we add a lot: the more we can add the more quickly we read.

These and many other points are discussed fully in the book by Smith that has already been recommended. For our present purposes all we need to remember is this: the ability to read fluently and well implies considerable linguistic sophistication. If a child has this sophistication then he is ready to begin reading. If he has not got it then he is not ready, and if we force him to try, he will almost certainly fail and begin to acquire negative attitudes of aversion, not only to reading, but probably also to school, which he will come to see as a place where he is made to feel uncomfortable and inferior. This linguistic sophistication is a very complex set of skills and attitudes. Among other things it involves:

(a) A desire to read, very often in imitation of parents and other adults or older children. This was mentioned briefly in Chapter 2.

(b) A feeling that reading is likely to be pleasant. Children are like adults: the things we like we do with enthusiasm; gardening and decorating (in my case anyway) tend to be neglected. It also involves the question of the benefit we think we are likely to get from expenditure of effort: we might make the effort to travel to another distant town to hear a famous pianist or pop group (depending on taste). We are unlikely even to cross the road to see an inferior film. We are likely to turn to books more readily in the future if books and words have been linked with pleasant experiences in the past than if we have repeatedly failed to make sense of some coverless, tatty and probably unhygienic reader.

(c) Favourable attitudes to language use itself. I was once carrying out some research into the language development of little children. I used 'nonsense' words linked with Disney-like pictures. Some children treated each new picture and word as the starting point for word-play, making up little rhymes or inventing stories about them. Sometimes they just commented, 'Huh, he's a funny looking chap. Whoever saw a duck with four legs?' etc. Other children were much more instrumental: they treated each word as a word and nothing more. Their answers were sometimes right and sometimes wrong, but they did not seem to see the situation as one calling for comment. Of course there were many reasons for this but there seemed to be quite a large relationship between the attitudes towards words of these children and their ability to read. Children in the first group, even though they were often less intelligent than those in the second group, had nearly all made a good beginning with reading. Many of the children in the second group, even though they were by no means dull, were often having difficulty with reading as late as nine years of age.

(d) Certain scanning habits are also necessary. Skilled readers do not begin to read at the beginning of a sentence and then work their way steadily through it. They tend to take in each group of words at a glance and their eyes move along the sentence in a series of jerks. More importantly they look back at what has gone before, often without realising it. There are many reasons for this. We have already shown that in order to understand a sentence we need a lot of prior knowledge. When we read we work from only a few cues in any sentence and reconstruct that sentence in our heads as we go along, adding (as has been shown) a lot from our own stores of knowledge. We look back, partly, to check that the cues we used at the beginning match those we are using at the end. Another reason is that, even when we are adult, our short-term memory is rather limited in the amount of information it can handle and pass on to our long-term memory, and it is the long-term memories that we use when we are interpreting speech and reading. We glance back, as it were, to 'top up' the information in our short-term memories so that they can pass a more complete message inwards to the long-term store. (Readers will have to take my word for it, but there is good evidence that we have at least two memories — short- and long-term — and possibly also a third, a mid-term memory. If the readers want details they will have to study a lot of psychology and then search for them through many rather tedious research journals.)

(e) We also need to have a knowledge not only of different words and of grammar, but also a lot of knowledge about the probabilities of occurrence of different combinations of words. This has already been discussed.

(f) Finally readers need to know a lot of social and other 'background' facts. Examples are not difficult to find: most of us have been in the situation where we feel we understand the words but still cannot grasp the ideas. Much of the thinking in this book is derived from the work of the Swiss psychologist Piaget. Many students and teachers find Piaget's work very difficult to read. It is not a question of the words he uses. Although some of them *are* strange they can be learned easily enough. Nor is it a question of the grammar, which is perfectly straightforward. It is more a question of understanding the philosophical problems that he is trying to answer. Unless the reader is well acquainted with European philosophy much of what Piaget is writing seems incomprehensible. The same applies to children: I have seen a student trying to read from *Paddington Bear* to a group of children from homes that were very poor, both financially and culturally. Many of the children came from immigrant families. Even if the children had understood the language it is questionable whether the middle-class whimsy that pervades the book meant anything to them. Most introductory readers seem to involve children from moderately rich, white, middle-class families, with large gardens. It may be that the conceptual strangeness adds an additional dimension of difficulty for some children trying to learn to read.

Although most children in nursery groups, playgroups and probably even the first year in many infants' schools are not yet ready for a formal introduction to reading, these years are of crucial importance. During this time, the children must have the experiences that give them the linguistic sophistication they will need in reading. In other words the work of teachers of very young children is not so much with reading as with language.

This language-development activity must always have two sides. On the one hand the children listen to the teacher talking; she tells stories and introduces new words and ideas. But we do not learn anything passively: no one will learn to be a concert pianist by merely reading a book about it, or even by listening to other concert pianists playing, valuable as these activities may be. If he wishes to succeed then he must devote hours of practice to his instrument. So too, children need to spend lots of time talking. The experienced teacher will complain that they never seem to stop talking in any case. This is true, but it is not the stereotyped, everyday, mindless gossip that is needed: they pick this up from home and in the playground. Often the youngest children sound like little old men and women enjoying a jolly good natter. It is a very different sort of language use that must be practised: the children must try to express themselves, to describe their feelings and what they have seen, to make explicit in words what is implicit in situations, to tell simple stories that will be interesting and exciting, because some words have been chosen and used rather than others, and so on. This is not as easy as it sounds. It will come only with continued practice, and from encouragement in a tolerant, understanding environment.

Throughout this book the importance of accompanying activities with language has been stressed. In this way the children can learn much essential new vocabulary. But language development is more than this. By talking to children and encouraging them to talk about what they have seen and done, the teacher can help them to arrange their thoughts in new ways and to make their thinking explicit. Socio-linguists have shown that there appear to be well-marked differences between children from different social backgrounds. Most children learn to use language fluently to express their ideas. They use what has been called an *elaborated code*. In an elaborated code children use a comparatively wide range of vocabulary. They use many more modifying words such as adjectives and adverbs. Their sentences are longer and more complex. But for many children from the poorest families this elaborated code is impossible. They tend to use, instead, a *restricted code*, in which only a limited set of words is available, and those which are used tend to be concrete. Sentences are short and simple and they often have difficulty in making their meaning clear in the absence of contextual cues. What is usually overlooked is that if a child habitually uses a restricted code then he will be unable to add much to sentences using the elaborated code used by teachers and found in books. One of the essential features of linguistic sophistication is missing.

Some other research workers have taken exception to the views that have just been outlined. It is probably true that some children are limited to mainly restricted codes of language, but the people who oppose this view feel that to say this implies some sort of inferiority. There is no implication of this at all. A restricted code may have many values in itself: it may express warmth and security and solidarity with one's family and friends. It may very often be strikingly vivid in some descriptions. But if it interferes with understanding of their teachers, if it delays their learning to read, if it shuts off from them much literature and scientific and mathematical thinking, then the children who can use and understand only restricted code are going to be at a serious disadvantage in education, and one that becomes increasingly more serious with the passage of time.

Now these children seem to acquire this limited sort of sophistication because their parents also use a restricted code. If teachers are aware of this then they can begin to remedy the position: by talking frequently to children about the interesting and exciting things that the children are involved in they will provide more elaborated models for them to observe. At first the sentences used must be simple. Long sentences and those involving many subordinate clauses must be avoided at first. Of course they must not be avoided all the time, or else the children will never get the opportunity to learn and use them. One particular grammatical form that should not be used frequently with any young children is the passive. There is much evidence that children misunderstand it. Thus if a teacher says or if a child reads: 'Mary was punched by John' the children often misinterpret this to mean it was Mary who did the punching and John who received the blow. Sometimes it does not matter very much but in some stories misunderstanding may make the whole story incomprehensible. The best thing to do is to use a passive sentence then repeat it in the active: 'Mary was punched by John. Wasn't he a naughty boy? He punched Mary.' In this way the children gradually come to recognise that the two sentence forms mean the same thing. Incidentally some children well into the secondary school stage appear to confuse this sort of sentence. They are probably regular users of a restricted code, and are often very poor readers.

The importance of stories as a focal point around which the day revolves has already been pointed out. Of course stories have many other values as well. In the first place stories act as a valuable means for transmitting to the next generation values and assumptions current in any culture. These stories are often about folk heroes (such as Robin Hood). Besides being exciting in themselves, they put before the children ideas about individual freedom, of the underdog standing up to the wicked rulers and usually winning. Other stories stress the values of honesty, frugality and obedience.

In the past, in some cultures, there were professional story tellers who would gather a crowd round them in a market place or under a tree and keep their listeners entertained by the hour. This sort of thing disappeared long ago in Britain, but until quite recently very useful sources of stories were grandparents. Today, however, grandparents are usually younger, frequently live at a distance from their married children and in many cases are working. As a result that source of stories has dried up. Many children in secondary schools today do not know the common fairy tales, nursery rhymes and so on, so the next generation is likely to be even more deprived of entertainment and experience essential for later learning in this simple way. There are signs that many children seem to be starved of the stimulus to imagination and thought that stories can give. In part this reflects the growing gap between generations that we discussed in Chapter 1. Clearly the nursery schools and playgroups have a very important role to play in this matter.

Stories have yet another important function to fulfil. By their means children are exposed to richer samples of language. It is in stories that teachers can gradually allow their pupils to become accustomed to listening to and understanding more complex sentences. The wise teacher also uses the stories to establish ideas and words that have occurred elsewhere. Perhaps one child has been experimenting with objects that sink and float. Later the teacher touches lightly on this topic in a story: perhaps the young hero has dropped something into the village pond and it has sunk. Casually in passing the teacher might say something like: 'And Mary knows lots of other things that sink in water, don't you Mary? Can you tell us some?' On one occasion the author heard a little boy use the word 'gravity' to his teacher. He had heard it at home and was proud of his new knowledge. Later the teacher brought it up in a story, asking 'Who knows what "gravity" means? You do, don't you, John? You tell us.' Johnny did and was proud to receive a word of commendation. In this way words become things that make you feel good: they are likely to be used again.

The last important function of stories has already been

touched on: they are a valuable vehicle for stimulating the imagination. Children often seem to identify themselves with the hero or heroine. When the hero suffers they experience a little of his sorrow, when he succeeds and is happy the children's faces lighten, and when he is brave their shirt buttons nearly pop off as their chests swell with pride.

Clearly then stories play a very important part in the early education of children. In one sense they are the verbal counterpart of gaining experience through play. It would be impossible to give a list of suitable stories. Each teacher or playgroup leader must make her own selections. In general it is the old, well-tried, traditional stories that are most suitable. The books (which should be displayed for the children to look at on low shelves arranged in one corner) should be colourful, clean and pleasant to handle. Their print should be well designed and should be quite large: some children will inevitably try to begin to read some words. They should have large, colourful and *uncluttered* illustrations. Sometimes the teacher will read them as straightforward stories, at other times she will edit them to make them more suitable for her own class, or to introduce material as advised earlier. In this case the book should always rest on her knees: if children are going to approach the difficult task of learning to read with enthusiasm then they must associate pleasant verbal experiences with actual books. After pairing books with pleasure in this way for some time, the books will come to elicit some of the pleasant feelings themselves: the children will have begun 'to like books'.

Teachers should not hesitate to compose their own stories. No great literary skill is necessary (although the more there is of it, the better) and there is probably not too much need for a vivid imagination: often the best kinds of story are those in which the children can identify with the hero, usually an animal or small boy or girl. The incidents are those that occur in every child's life – helping mother, going shopping, going away for holidays, being naughty, getting lost and getting into trouble and so on.

However, some teachers may not feel able to make up their own stories, especially if they are just beginning to teach and are uncertain of themselves and their skills. Luckily there is a whole host of readily available stories: the Old Testament, myths and legends, especially from the ancient world, such as the adventures of Odysseus, the Trojan War or the search for the Golden Fleece. On many occasions when I was teaching severely deaf children aged seven and eight, but with the language development of much younger children, I took the subjects of my daily story sessions from these sources as well as from the stories of Tristan and Isolde, the medieval French epics such as the *Chanson de Roland* and many others. I prepared some illustrations in advance to help extend the understanding of my handicapped children and introduced them into their subsequent playing. One of my pupils, a very severely deaf boy who was also educationally subnormal and who was unable to use or understand any but the simplest language, on one occasion brought into class cuttings from the local newspaper on the film *Helen of Troy*. By means of gestures and a few words he showed that he remembered much of the story, greatly to my surprise. I had forgotten telling the story, but had done so well over a term before. If a story could have this effect on a severely retarded boy, who must have been able to understand only a small fraction of the language (much less, probably, than the average three-year-old) and the ideas that were being used, what impact could it have on a bright, lively child with all his faculties?

In addition to stories there are many other valuable language activities that must find their way into the daily life of children in nursery schools and classes: simple songs, nursery rhymes, movement games accompanied by words, Christmas carols and so on. Once more, great sophistication is not needed: simple songs with repetitive choruses, accompanied wherever possible by large, chunky movements are just what is needed. Sometimes it helps if one of the teachers or a helper can play the piano or guitar, or one of them can tap rhythmically on a tambourine.

So far in discussing the language development and pre-reading activities, informality has been stressed. It must be emphasized again that at this stage any sort of formal work in these fields is entirely out of place for most, and probably all, children. When children are listening to a story, the teacher must be prepared to break off and modify it if one of the children makes a comment or asks a question: it is often very useful to incorporate the children's own ideas into stories. It is also important to allow the children to sit or lie comfortably. During a story session the teacher usually sits on a low chair or pile of cushions and the children form a group round her. Some will use chairs, others the floor, so, if possible, the floor should be covered with carpet. Some of the children will listen raptly, sucking their thumbs or twiddling their hair, others will fiddle with some toy, while yet others may appear not to be interested at all. On one occasion I watched a little boy who refused to sit down and listen to the student who was telling a story (the Paddington Bear story already referred to). Instead he crawled about under a table playing with a car. In conversation afterwards, however, it became apparent that he was one of the few children who had actually understood most of the story! It takes time for children to get used to sitting still, and at times even the best seems to get the fidgets. Unless the behaviour actually disrupts the story or interferes with the enjoyment of the rest of the children it is best in these cases to ignore the wriggles. A child who is a frequent disrupter can sit close to the teacher: as soon as unwelcome behaviour begins a restraining hand placed gently on his head or shoulder often has a calming effect. If the behaviour is totally disruptive then it is probably better to have one of the assistants remove the child and to engage him in something more interesting to him. In this way he does not hinder the other children and their obvious enjoyment usually does much more to improve the behaviour of the naughty child than any reprimand or nagging on the part of the teacher.

In other chapters some mention has been made of informal introductions to reading during other activities. The artistic productions of children, for example, can be labelled with their names, but no great stress should be laid on this. This practice has two advantages: it identifies each child's work, so that when the time comes to take it home to show parents and other relatives, there are no squabbles about who each picture belongs to. In addition it helps to build up the idea that words are useful labels. This can be a real step forward especially for the child who grows up in a non-reading home and who may genuinely not understand what reading is about. A useful intermediate step towards identifying themselves with a symbol (which is, after all, what their names are) is to mark each child's belongings with a picture: thus one child's towel hangs under a picture of a yellow rabbit. In the cloakroom his coat and hat also hang under a similar picture, and so on.

Some children, especially the older ones, may be on the verge of beginning to read and some teachers may wish to help them through the early stages. There is a lot of controversy about whether the children use a *phonic* method (learning the different sounds of letters and building up words), from these elements or whether they should use *word or sentence wholes* and so on. Most of these arguments have little real value: the teacher can pay her money and take her pick. Whatever method she uses, some children will succeed and others will not. However, Smith (in the book mentioned earlier) presents evidence to show that the processes of interpreting letters, words and sentences or phrases are in fact different from each other. It is probable that to learn the letters first and then laboriously to put them together is likely to delay reading. In the first place many of the English words cannot be put together in this way: 'elephant', 'aeroplane' and many others are good examples. More seriously, the limitations on our short-term memories will mean that after we have identified the first five letters or so, we will forget the earliest ones as we go on to spell out the remainder. In addition children's language is not organised in a 'letter' sort of way. Many young children have difficulty in sorting out individual words from a sentence, let alone 'letters' which do not occur even as units in the way words do. They tend to think in 'wholes'. Therefore, if the children are to use what they already know of English to help their understanding of what they are trying to read, they must be able to perform this in the only way available to them. They must use a sentence-whole method.

In this case any work in reading should be done on an individual basis. At first the teacher should go through the reading book looking at the pictures and talking about them with the child, encouraging him to make comments and pointing out features that are significant. These features will be those that the text specifically mentions. A second stage of this instruction should preferably consist of the child telling the story of the book in his own words to the teacher, a helper or any other available adult bystander. By this time the child is ready to make the essential personal contribution to the reading. Now the teacher can go through the book again, reading each sentence and encouraging the child to repeat it after her. Not too much should be attempted at any one time. Little and often is much better than long sessions once a week. The child will probably not be reading in the true sense of the word: at best he will be remembering what the teacher read, and adding other bits that he knows.

Let us try to see what the child is doing psychologically at this time. We know that when we read we do not read every word. Instead we work from a number of relevant clues, called 'features'. It is probable that each of us tends to use rather different features. As we learned to read we gradually worked out for ourselves on the basis of our experience which features were important and which not. Thereafter we use these features. Some of us use the most significant and parsimonious set of features: we become skilled, fluent, rapid readers. But others may very well select different sets of features, whose use is less efficient. More effort is needed to interpret the sentence using these features, and as a result the reading is slower and less fluent. In everyday terms we say that we have acquired bad reading habits.

An example may make this clearer. One day I was taking one of my young deaf pupils for a 'reading' lesson. I realise now that I was wasting my time since the child was nowhere near ready for reading, but he was quite bright and had begun to sort out for himself some of the features necessary for interpreting a passage. In this case he had come to realise that only parts of words were necessary to establish the basic meaning. We came across a sentence about a child in school: 'The teacher asked John to tidy up the classroom. John rubbed the blackboard clean.' The deaf boy looked baffled by this. He could 'read' the sentences in the sense that he could pronounce the words fairly well, yet something was worrying him. He was asked to demonstrate the meaning of what he had read. He did this, using words, signs and natural gestures, indicating that John had gone to sleep in the classroom. The author asked him to show how he had arrived at this strange conclusion. Very carefully he covered half of the word 'rubbed' with his finger. Only part of the word was necessary, remember, to establish the basic meaning. Unfortunately he covered up the first three letters 'rub', leaving 'bed' to provide the clue as to the meaning. This sort of mistake could probably only occur with a deaf child who had never heard the essential similarity of pronunciation between 'rub' and 'rubbed', but analogous mistakes are not infrequent with normally hearing children. It would probably be more useful to the teacher to regard them *not* merely as mistakes but as a necessary psychological step towards learning to read. The results may be wrong but the method is healthy.

We see therefore that if we expose children to a written stimulus they will gradually work out for themselves the set of distinctive features necessary for them to interpret the passage. At present we do not know much about what these features are. Later when we know more we may be able to help children to acquire them more efficiently and systematically. However, we do know that the distinctive features that we use to interpret letters, words and sentences are very earlier statement that to learn letters before words or sentences may actually slow down the process of learning to sentences may actually slow down the process of learning to read: children are using an inappropriate set of distinctive features for the task in hand.

One of the first distinctive features that children learn to isolate for themselves is probably the overall pattern of the

letter or word. Thus,

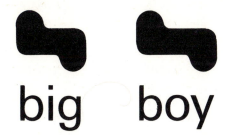

These represent the shapes of the letters

look rather similar, and may be confused in early stages of learning to read. On the contrary,

present very different patterns and are less likely to be confused. The importance of this shape recognition suggests a useful pre-reading game that grows naturally out of other matching games that have been discussed earlier. The teacher could prepare large numbers of sets of cards containing different shapes:

These shapes are based on the words 'dog', 'daddy' and 'mummy'. Each shape needs to be duplicated, and the task the children have is to match each of the cards they have with a stimulus card. Since speed is important in the interpreting process of reading, the older children can be taught to play 'snap' using the cards.

At the letter level, matching cards can also be used. As before, duplicate sets of cards to be matched should be prepared for the children to use. The letters should be written in bold characters, and may contain not only lower- and upper-case letters, but also non-letter shapes. It must be remembered here that it is not the letters themselves that are being taught but habits of discriminating rapidly between small features.

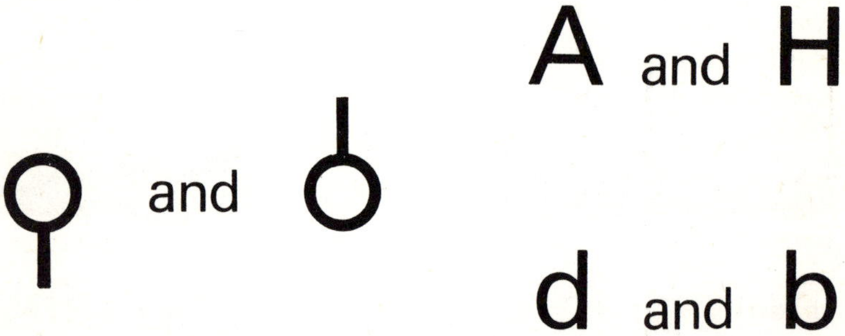

A and H

ϙ and ♂

d and b

Another skill that is essential for reading English is the habit of working from left to right. This is not natural: other societies do the reverse. Evidence from the common confusions of little children, for instance,

no ～ on

saw ～ was

of ～ for

suggest that they do not at first perceive differences between right and left or up and down. When this confusion is carried to the 'word' level, it is not uncommon for children to read 'no' as 'on', or 'dog' as 'god'. (Incidentally, when mistakes such as this are frequent it warns us that the children have been actually *mistaught* to read. They have not been taught or encouraged to contribute what they already know to the interpretative process. If they were doing this then they would not read like this: 'He — s — saw — was — sit — sitting — no — on the — what's that word?' (I have actually heard this.) Confusion between 'saw' and 'was' is not so serious a mistake here: both could occur after 'He', but 'no' is right out of place: it is extremely unlikely that the child would ever *say* it. Clearly he *knows* that it could not occur normally, but presumably reading for him is so meaningless that he has given up using what he knows and so makes nonsense of the message. Certainly, by the time he reached the end he would have been thoroughly confused. This is not reading.

What is needed to prevent the acquisition of bad perceptive habits is a lot of pre-reading experience in looking from left to right. This can be done by sticking sequences of pictures on to cards, shuffling them up and getting the children to put them in the correct order to tell a story. A simple home-made frame can be used, consisting of a sheet of hardboard with thin raised pieces stuck on as follows:

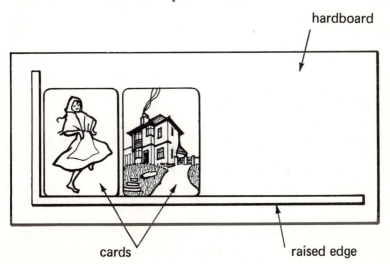

The children are shown how to put the first picture right into the corner, the second next to it and so on. The sequences should be very simple at first, but become gradually longer and more complex. Children's comics can be cut up and the individual pictures from any strip stuck on separate cards. This saves the teacher a lot of time and provides material that the children are already used to. When the child has finished putting the pictures in sequence he should talk about the story he has made to the teacher or a helper. At first some of the sequences will be wrong, and this is further evidence of the way in which children's outlooks are different from those of adults. Sequences and the idea of cause and effect seem to be poorly developed in young children. This kind of error is not important in this activity: we are not trying to teach logical thought, merely to help the child adopt habits of looking that will be useful to him later when he begins to learn to read seriously.

In this chapter many different suggestions have been made about the importance of language in general and the overriding need for abundant language experience before children begin to read formally. A large number of suggestions as to actual activities have been provided. Little specific advice can be given: what teachers do will depend very much on their imaginations and on the resources available. The main problem outstanding is how these different activities are to be fitted into the rather short working day of young children. This point will be discussed briefly in the final chapter.

It is appropriate to end this rather lengthy chapter with a very important truth, taken from *Understanding Reading* by Frank Smith (p.55):

> The picture that has been presented shows a child from the very beginning of his life looking for rules that will provide him with the key to the language community in which he finds himself. The child has rules for learning rules, and he tests to see which particular rules apply. We shall see that precisely the same kind of argument may be applied to reading — that basically a child is equipped with every skill that he needs in order to read and to learn to read: all that he needs to discover is the particular rules that apply.

8 Learning about ourselves

In Chapter 6 it was shown how, through playing, working and growing in a stable, challenging environment, children can learn to know themselves as individuals within a social setting. But they need to learn more about themselves than this. It is at this time that young children begin to acquire the fundamentals of personal knowledge and habits of later full citizenship. In this chapter we shall look at a number of activities through which the children can begin to learn about themselves, their bodies and health, and about the world around them.

As in so many other fields it is not a matter of formal teaching at this stage. Young children do not learn about health as a 'subject' in the usual school sense. Instead they come to acquire valuable, health-promoting habits linked wherever possible with verbal explanation. Much of the day in a nursery class, playgroup or infants' school is devoted to regular routine activities: drinking the daily ration of milk, eating an apple after lunch, sleeping, playing in the open air, washing hands after using the lavatory and so on. The children soon pick up the elements of this regular routine, and, like so many other aspects of education at this early stage, the teacher and her helpers will take advantage of the activities to talk about them and explain why they are good for us. On a cold day the teacher will see that the children wrap up warmly before going out to play. She will encourage the children to move about to keep warm. Inevitably these activities will give rise to questions from the children: why our hearts beat when we have been running, why we get out of breath, why 'smoke' comes out of our nostrils on a cold day. Explanations are given incidentally and naturally. Their value is increased because they grow out of the children's activities and curiosity.

Sometimes the children will fall and bruise themselves or cut their knees or hands. Once again, as the teacher washes the cut, rubs on some soothing antiseptic ointment and dispenses comfort and reassurance, she will talk about germs and the need for cleanliness, as well as the dangers of carelessness.

Within the general framework of the school day children will need appropriate physical activity: physical education in the modern meaning of the term. I have seen five- and six-year-old children standing in rows doing the old-fashioned 'physical jerks'. Fortunately this was not in an English school, and it cannot be emphasised strongly enough that this sort of activity has no place whatever in the modern education of young children. For them physical education should be conceived in terms of using the whole body: playing in the open air if the weather is suitable, running, crawling, jumping, trying to hop and so on. The best kind of physical activity is that which occurs naturally in play in which they are exercising many muscles and breathing in a relaxed way. But where, for whatever reason, this free play movement cannot take place, then the teacher may have to set up a more artificial situation. If the weather is cold or wet, the physical education sessions should be indoors, although this may be difficult to arrange, especially in some playgroups where space is limited. Many nursery school and infants' classes have a verandah outside the classrooms: the children can play outside and keep dry, even when it is raining. Whenever possible the children should be encouraged to strip down to their pants and knickers, running about in bare feet or wearing plimsolls if there is any danger of splinters or stones. It is often very useful to have some simple music to accompany the activity. At the very least a tambourine or drum can be beaten. The teacher varies the rhythm and the children move appropriately, inventing heavy slow steps for one rhythm, running lightly on their toes for another. To the accompaniment of her tambourine the teacher can encourage the children to move jerkily or smoothly, to crouch or leap up, and so on.

If one of the teachers can play the piano or a guitar then simple real music can be used to accompany the movement sessions, and in this case greater variety of stimulus can be achieved. The BBC schools broadcasts include 'Music and Movement' programmes which are of great value. At the very least beginning teachers may pick up some useful tips from these programmes. They also unfortunately have some drawbacks. One activity may have caught the interest of the children and the teacher may feel that it would be better to spend more time on it. But programme time is limited and the broadcast must be completed on schedule. Another problem is that the timing of the broadcast may not fit in with the school programme: the movement broadcast may clash with some other equally valuable activity. Finally, it is not impossible that the teacher may have her class ready for a programme, only to discover that the radio does not work. She is then left with the problem of planning a programme for the children 'off the cuff'. Some of these lessons can be very creative, especially if the teacher is experienced, but in that case she probably would not be using the BBC to help her out. In this last sort of emergency, most teachers usually have an alternative set of activities up their sleeves, so that no time is wasted. The other problems can be overcome quite simply by taping programmes on a portable tape-recorder, and using them a day or two later. The teacher can listen to them before using them with her class, so that she can prepare her class for the activity. It is then relatively easy to replay some activity that the children like or that the teacher thinks is useful. While the children are busy following the tape-recorder, the teacher can make comments and praise the children who are trying hard or who demonstrate 'good ideas', and can keep an eye on the odd juvenile criminal who, for reasons best known only to himself, seems intent on wrecking the enjoyment of other children.

Once again the teacher should call reinforcing techniques into play. Many children are as uncreative in movement as in other things. They may repetitively carry out a few stereo-typed movements, or they may blindly copy other more imaginative children. This is inevitable, but still it is better to try to involve the children, to help as many as possible gain the confidence to experiment for themselves. The teacher who knows her children will be on the alert for the child who after a long period of rather dull work suddenly tries out something new. This is the time for the quiet word of commendation accompanied by a smile. Gradually the child becomes aware of the pleasures of experiment. As the experiment is linked with positive reinforcement, the tendency to experiment will itself in turn become re-inforcing. The child will gradually acquire the confidence to experiment still more and will come to 'like' the movement sessions in and for themselves.

Sometimes it is a useful practice to commend a child publicly. Perhaps a little girl has tried to crawl up and over a small vaulting 'horse' in a new way. When this happens the teacher can stop the activity and ask the girl to show the rest of the class. Most young children seem to like this occasional public commendation, and they will certainly throw them-selves with renewed vigour and enthusiasm into the activities. Other children will be able to try the activity for themselves, and several will extend the new ideas still further. But the teacher must be careful: some children are shy and find public attention painful. Only expérience and personal sensitivity can give guidance in this matter.

Some simple apparatus is needed even at this early stage. Children need a frame to climb on, and it must be big enough to allow them to swing on it. They need somewhere to jump from and something to crawl under. The best way to use this apparatus is to allow the children freedom to experiment, merely telling them to think of as many ways as possible of, say, climbing over the frame, and reinforcing individuals where appropriate. If children are to jump down from a frame, or even to roll about on the ground, then some form of large soft mat is necessary.

In addition to these general body-exercises, little children need opportunities to extend their physical skills. Benches can be used for practising balancing as they walk. They also need to practise hopping, jumping with feet together and careful placing of their feet as they walk. These skills can, as in so many other cases, most usefully be practised in games. Hula hoops placed near each other on the floor can form 'islands'. The children hop or jump from one to the other. At other times they become stepping stones and the children can play at crossing crocodile-infested rivers quickly and smoothly.

Many children, even as old as five, have difficulty in catching, throwing and kicking with accuracy. There should also be a supply of large soft balls that the children can roll, kick and throw to each other. Home-made bean-bags (simple bags of brightly coloured material, filled with dried peas) are also popular.

Although the youngest children discussed in this book will lack the necessary skills, many young boys and girls are very keen to copy their older brothers and sisters. The girls will try, as they get older, to begin skipping. In this case the teacher can introduce them to some simple exercises. Two people hold a rope, one at each end. At first the children jump over the rope held low to the ground. Later it is swung gently from side to side for the children to practise a rather more difficult activity involving timing. After this, real skipping can be attempted. Some of the boys will probably try to 'play football'. They will not really be able to play, because very few at this age know the rules, and many may not even realise that rules exist! But groups of boys (and girls sometimes) may kick a ball round. There is no competition in the real sense, it is merely a boisterous activity of great value. The children learn to run and swerve, to kick with one foot while balancing on the other. They will bump into each other and be knocked to the ground. Sometimes there will be tears, but for most of the time everyone enjoys himself. The composition of the 'teams' usually changes: new children join in while others drop out to go off and do other interesting things. If there is enough of it available, it is always useful to keep a patch of land free for this kind of activity. Care is needed to keep the smaller children away: a five-year-old is pretty small to an adult, but to a rather timid and fearful three-year-old he may appear positively elephantine.

The activities described have focused on developing skills through games, first the gross bodily skills and then the finer problems of control of the hands and arms. Now we will look at games that can help to increase the dexterity of hands and fingers. This order is important, since it is the way in which development occurs naturally. Children master gross, large-scale skills first. then gradually move on to those that require finer discrimination. Care is needed in introducing the different levels of activity: the sort of skill that is being practised must be relevant to the stage of development of the children. Sometimes the teacher will have to intervene and steer individuals in one direction rather than another, but often the question of choice can safely be left to the children themselves. If a number of different activities is available children will soon find the one they can do best and are happiest with. If they are carefully watched over a period of time they can be seen, at first rather timidly, trying something new and more difficult. They will probably leave it very soon, but later return to it. In this way their skills increase and their self-confidence grows steadily.

Many of the activities that the children engage in during their playing, working and growing will provide practice in fine control of fingers. Jig-saw puzzles at different levels of difficulty are always popular. At first they consist of a colourful picture with a few shapes cut out. Each cut-out part will have a small handle so that the children can pick it up. At first the child will take the pieces out and put them back. Later he may be given the board with pieces already out: his task now is to recognise where each goes and fit it in. To an adult this can appear trivial, but it often stretches young children, both perceptually (they must recognise the shape and match it with a space) and manually (having recognised where the piece goes, they have to orientate it properly, which often defeats them). Later on the jig-saws will come closer to the normal commerical ones. They should be made of simple pictures on thick wood and carved into a few simple shapes, preferably not interlocking, since at this stage the problem of locking shapes together is usually beyond the dexterity of the children. As the children grow older and gain more experience they are able to cope with thinner pieces cut into smaller shapes, but as a general principle the pictures to be built should be well within the conceptual limits of the users. All adult jig-saw puzzles and many supposedly designed for children that can be bought cheaply at local newsagents' shops are completely unsuitable: the pieces are too small and complicated while the pictures are too adult and cluttered. If no suitable jig-saw puzzles can be found, or if money is in short supply (especially in playgroups), then puzzles can be made at home. Bright colourful pictures of everyday scenes (a bus and other traffic, a seaside scene, a farmyard) are carefully stuck on to plywood. The surface should be varnished to preserve it, then a simple fret-saw is used to cut the picture into shapes. To help with this it is usually better to trace the lines of the cut in pencil on the back. Many fathers or older brothers are pleased to be asked to contribute to the class's stock in this way.

There are also many different 'finger games' available. In these the teacher and children sing a song, which is usually simple and repetitive. As they sing they point to items, clap their hands, touch different parts of their bodies, wriggle their heads, hands, fingers and so on. Most children find these very enjoyable and they can be used to fill in odd gaps in the day's activity.

Music can also be pressed into use. Its place as an accompaniment to gross movement has already been discussed, but there are many musical activities that can contribute to the finer control of hands and fingers. Children can clap to the rhythm of songs. Even where there is no music available practice can be gained in clapping to the rhythm of their names: 'George' gets one big, boisterous clap, 'Caroline' has three quick taps. When the children are singing nursery rhymes they can also clap to the rhythm, by no means an easy task for young children. If there is a supply of drums, tomtoms, tambourines, triangles and cymbals, and if the children have never used these instruments before, the first few times are likely to be concussive to all adults within earshot. This is inevitable: the children have seen films of military bands, they have probably been exposed to noisy pop music on television or record players. No one can blame them for doing what many adults and larger brothers and sisters do. Unfortunately when the noise becomes too loud other teachers or neighbours may complain, and when this happens the instruments may be put away, never to be used again. This is a pity for two reasons. In the first place they are expensive, and in times when money is scarce we cannot afford to have our money locked up in an unusable form. More importantly, with continued experience the children grow through the early noisy stages, and then the instruments contribute to their manual control, as they learn to hit their drum or triangle in time, and sometimes to wait doing nothing.

Where a teacher or parent has some musical training, even small children can be led to make real music. There are commerically produced chime bars, glockenspiels and so on, and with ingenuity they can be made from simple materials at home. Those associated with the work of Carl Orff are skilfully designed around the pentatonic scale (the 'black' notes of the piano). Once the children have learned to control their hands rhythmically they can begin to make music. The advantage of the pentatonic scale is that it is impossible to make unpleasant discordant sounds because they always sound in tune. Thus children move on from the purely percussive type of music towards melodic music: an older child can 'play a tune' while the others keep time. Sometimes a teacher may play a melody on the guitar while the children accompany her on their instruments. I have seen skilled and sensitive teachers gradually lead their young pupils (some as young as five years old) to plan their own music, including use of elementary notation. Through activities like those outlined here the children had acquired the necessary control and group discipline to make music together. They were also beginning to read musical notation, which the teacher wrote on a large blackboard as the children made different suggestions.

Although in this chapter the emphasis has been laid on using music and movement as vehicles for other aspects of development, it must not be assumed that these activities have no value in themselves. What is being sought here is a new orientation. Some teachers, especially beginners, feel that 'music' must be something formal and difficult: that something must be learned. In this they are probably transferring memories of their own childish experiences in learning to 'play the piano', where they tried to learn such useful tips as 'Every good boy deserves favour' for the 'lines' of the treble staff, or where they fumbled their way through

five-finger exercises. These activities *can* be valuable, but they
have no place in the early stages. If music comes initially to
be seen as some pleasurable activity then the mechanical
aspects can be quickly learned later.

However, it is a fact that our own experience exerts such a
powerful influence on us it is often better to try a totally
new way if we wish to change things. This new way is never
achieved by simply re-jigging the old matter and searching
after flashy gimmicks. It is more likely to be found by
adopting a fundamentally new viewpoint. The viewpoint
outlined here is that music may, for little children, be
introduced as a game ancillary to some pleasurable activity.
In this way music itself takes on some of the pleasures
associated with the other activity, and because there is no
hint of formal practice, the children throw themselves into it
with gusto.

So far we have looked at activities that help the children
not only to improve their bodily skills and to develop certain
healthy habits, but also to lay the foundations for continuing
them by explaining, in passing and informally, the reasons
why these things are necessary and good for us. The children
must also be made aware of the wider world around them.
Once more this must be done informally. The world of
nature is constantly fascinating to children, and in a properly
organised educational system they will enjoy the opportunities to observe things, to listen to stories about them and to
talk about them to their teachers, parents and to each other.

The passage of the seasons is always with us. On some days
there is rain, on others snow or winds. The teacher can talk
about these different phenomena, sometimes giving a simple
explanation, at others reading or telling a story or poem.
When the wind is boisterous outside the children can mimic it
in their music and movement sessions: whirling round across
the floor or playground like leaves picked up and tossed here
and there. One word of warning is needed here: some
teachers (probably because they do not really understand the
matter themselves) believe that a true explanation is too
difficult for little children. They often oversimplify and
unwittingly make subsequent correct learning more difficult.
For example children should never be told that rain comes

from clouds that bump together, or that clouds pick up water as they cross the sea. If we tell them this then be sure they will learn it. You may be sure too that learning at this stage is often very resistant to later change. I once met an intelligent well-motivated fifteen-year-old boy who was having great difficulty in learning the necessary facts of meteorology for his GCE geography examination. It appeared, after questioning, that he had once been told that the clouds had picked up water in crossing the sea. Later he had gone to the seaside for a holiday and had felt the spray from breaking waves on his face. Trying to understand things, as all children do, he had equated these two 'facts', and believed that rain was nothing more than spray. His problem was that he could not understand how spray could go right into the air (he had flown in an aeroplane several times and seen raindrops on the windows). This early learning and the internal model that he had constructed to integrate it with other experience were so powerful that he literally could barely understand what his geography master was trying to explain.

The true fact is that clouds do not pick up water: they *are* water. The water has evaporated from a sea or lake and has become a gas. As a result of certain physical changes in the atmosphere this invisible gas has condensed and become visible: a cloud has formed. Later rain falls (although physicists are not completely sure how this comes about!). If a teacher does not understand this process or cannot explain it sufficiently simply then it is better for her to leave it alone altogether. The conclusion is straightforward. If anyone is to try to educate children he or she should be well educated herself. Although it is contrary to much contemporary wisdom both inside and outside the teaching profession, the younger the children and the greater the simplification needed, the more the teacher needs to understand. I have myself taught university students, grammar school sixth-formers and handicapped children of nursery and infant-school ages. I am convinced that it is the younger children who make the greater demands on the teacher, both in terms of professional skills and intellect. In a sixth form the pupils are at least as intelligent and sophisticated as the teacher. Sometimes indeed they may outshine him. They can read, they have access to libraries and can (and do) argue with their teachers when lesson material seems to conflict with experience and reading. Much of their education is in their own hands. A mediocre teacher can get away with a lot if he is teaching intelligent seventeen or eighteen year olds. Little children depend almost entirely for information on their teachers and parents. If the teacher feels unable to teach the right information then it is probably better not to attempt it at all. It is better merely to let them experience things and talk about them in the most general terms.

In addition to seasonal and meterological facts nursery classes can supply many other interesting experiences. If a teacher has a dog then he is called on to do his part: children see him panting and can learn about their own perspiration, they can take him for walks and learn about animal care informally. A big shaggy dog is often pleasant to snuggle up against and can give comfort to small children when they are upset. Other animals are often found in schools: gerbils, hamsters, rabbits, stick insects and fish are the regulars, while different seasons bring in tadpoles and sticklebacks. Feeding the animals, cleaning them, changing their water, making sure that they are cared for over weekends and holidays (which often calls for a complicated rota) provide opportunities for learning and talking as well as for acquiring habits of responsibility. With animals in the classroom, pregnancy and birth become ordinary everyday facts, to be talked about when they occur, then to be forgotten.

Most schools too have plants around them: bulbs are planted in spring, peas and mustard seed germinate and grow, collections of autumnal leaves are made and used in collage work, and so on. As before the teacher uses each experience as a starting point for informal teaching: talking about the needs of plants for warmth, water and light, or about why leaves die and fall off the trees in autumn. Teachers or a helper may plant bulbs, seeds, seedlings or shrubs in the garden around the school or playgroup 'hut'. The children should share in this activity, and the adult can talk about warmth and moisture, about needs for air and light. Each child can plant his own bulb and feel the warm dampness of the newly dug soil. On subsequent days children can help the teacher water the plants.

As well as learning about themselves and the world of
nature, the children have many other activities to sample.
They can help to tidy away the mess they have made while
painting or playing with the water-table. Sand spilled on the
floor can be swept up. One should not expect a perfect adult
standard to be reached, although even very young children
can be assiduous in helping. It is the general social model of
individuals helping each other and caring for the environment
that is of value. The activities available can go well beyond
cleaning chores: the children in many schools take it in turns
to help lay the table for lunch, or the bigger children help put
out the low camp-beds on which the children will have their
afternoon sleep. Very often they can help in simple food
preparation. With the cooperation of the cook, the children
can make pastry tarts and rock cakes. Under the guidance of
the teacher they learn to wash their hands, prepare and weigh
the ingredients, then mix them together. They take the 'raw'
cakes to the kitchen where the cook allows them to feel the
warmth from the oven. When the cooking time is up they go
back to watch the cakes being taken out of the oven, to smell
them and thank the cook for her help while they wait for the
products to cool sufficiently to be eaten. At other times
simple sweets can be made: most children like to make
chocolate toffee apples, peppermint creams, coconut ice and
so on. If a party is planned then some at least of the jellies
and trifles should be made with the help of the children, even
if the help consists of little more than each child giving a few
stirs to the mixture in a bowl. Of course, many children will
be gaining this valuable experience at home, but some will
not, especially if their mothers are working or have large
families. Unfortunately this communal sort of activity is
often time-consuming: it is quicker for the teacher to make
the cakes and jellies herself. The tendency to do this should
be resisted: apart from the learning that goes on, such
experiences capture the interest of the children and each one
can be pressed into the service of education: the children can
touch the jelly cubes, feeling their slipperiness and rubbery
quality. They can see the jelly dissolving in the boiling water,
and are often surprised to see the mixture slowly harden. All

of this should be accompanied by conversation. At appropriate times the need for cleanliness and the dangers of being scalded or burned, or of sharp knives and scissors, can be stressed, and the children learn to wait their turn at the exciting new activity.

The activities that have been briefly outlined so far will enable the young children to grow to understand themselves as individuals and as members of their families, and it will give them some insights into the natural world around them. They need also to begin to learn something of the social world that surrounds them. Just as most of the suggestions that have been given in this book should be seen not only as valuable in their own right but also as laying the foundations for more formal work later on, the activities to be discussed now will prove indispensable for subsequent work in geography and history, when the children are more mature. The aim of these subjects is to describe and study the lives of people and conditions in different lands and at different times. This can only be achieved if the children have enjoyed a firm basis of personal experience with which they can compare more exotic topics. Partly this comes down to the sheer problem of teaching the children 'to use their eyes', or more correctly of making them aware of their surroundings. Because most of us today live in urban environments where one street looks very much like another, and because we travel in cars, buses and trains that iron out many of the hills and valleys, it seems as though children grow up oblivious of the physical world around them. I have known children deny the existence of hills and valleys between Newbury and Oxford, even though they had frequently crossed the rolling Berkshire downs in coaches and cars. Others, when their attention was drawn to a field of wheat next to the road along which they walked to school every morning, seemed scarcely able to believe that there were fields there (rather than houses and gardens) let alone that it was a cereal crop rather than grass or potatoes!

In part this lack of observation stems from the more immediate interests that the children had when going to and from school: playing about, gossiping and so on, but a more serious cause is that of wrong teaching at all levels. It is not

uncommon to see quite young children learning about
Eskimos and pygmies. Apart from the fact that most of the
facts these lessons are based on are out of date, they teach
the children to think of such exciting things as geography as
being 'in books' and confined to the classroom, instead of
being all around them. Even adults sometimes find it difficult
to imagine themselves as part of geography and history.

These problems can be solved to some extent in the classes
and schools for the youngest children. Many children go
shopping with their mothers, but mothers are often too busy
thinking about what food to buy for the evening meal what
material to buy for a new dress or the gossip they are looking
forward to with their next-door neighbour, to be able to talk
to their child about the different goods they see and the
different people they meet. My own childhood memories and
current observation suggest that in these circumstances little
children tend to get very bored. Yet they are missing valuable
opportunities for learning about the world, for learning new
words, for smelling coffee and tea, touching things and so on.
It is very useful in a playgroup or nursery class for the
teacher to go shopping occasionally during working hours. It
may be that something is needed for the school, or it may be
her own family shopping, but if she takes a few children with
her, she can talk to them, explain things and encourage them
to ask for items.

Young children are also keenly interested in people and
the work they do, especially the more visible types of work.
If there is a building site nearby, it is often possible to get
permission to take a group of children to visit the site, to let
them look at the foundations and excavations, lift up and
feel the rough textures of bricks and wood, talk to the
workmen and say 'thank you' when leaving. Most workmen
are very helpful and like to explain to the children what they
are doing. At the same time the teacher can point out
dangers, and impress on the children the seriousness of
trespassing on building sites in evenings and at weekends.

Almost every local adult occupation can receive its share
of attention: when the children visit the park they can talk to
the keeper picking up litter. He can tell them how much
there is of it, and how much nicer it is not to leave litter

about. The signs are that this sort of immediate experience
has much greater impact than any lesson or exhortation in
the classroom. (The main drawback of classroom talks about
such things as litter and road safety is that the children come
to see it as having relevance to the classroom and nowhere
else. After all, much of what goes on in a school does not go
on outside. As a result we may be unconsciously linking
certain activities with certain places and thus restricting their
wider application.) In the park, too, the children can make
acquaintance with the man cutting the grass. They can
examine the gang mower and look at the blades, to the
accompaniment of squeaks and groans. The man can show
them notches in the blades caused by stones and tins left on
the grass, and may even have bits of balls and dolls cut into
pieces by the mower. Once more some valuable social
learning is taking place.

Children often find postmen fascinating and, with a certain
amount of careful forward planning, it is possible to arrive at
a letter box with a real letter to post at the same time as the
postman comes to empty it. He will usually allow the
children to look inside, and show them how he changes the
day and time indicator for collections. Children are often
very keen on accuracy in this sort of situation. One class of
'bottom' infants had been doing a project on letters. Each
had chosen one of his paintings to send to a friend. In turn
the children came and told the teacher who they wanted to
send the letter to and she provided them with a copy of the
name and address, which they laboriously copied out on to
the envelope. Most of the children had brought a stamp from
home, but stamps were provided for those who had forgotten. Then the children went down to the nearest postbox,
put their letters in and waited for the postman to come. They
were very excited to see their own letters inside the box
(which suggests something to us about their thought processes: what did they think happened to the letters once they
were in the box? We adults assumed they knew). Several of
the children, however, insisted that the postman was not a
real postman. Questioning elicited the basis of their
misgivings: every postman they had seen in pictures during
their project had been wearing a peaked cap. This one was

not. He had left it in his van. However, he good naturedly
went to the van to put his cap on and the children were
satisfied. Suspicion was allayed.

If teachers are planning to carry out little projects and
activities like this it is best to think ahead. Make acquaintance with the postman or parkkeeper and explain when you
will be coming and what you hope the children will see. Most
people like to demonstrate their expertise and will often put
themselves out to a surprising extent. I once took a group of
children, rather older, but fairly severely retarded intellectually, on a visit to the local railway station. They were
allowed into the cab of the diesel locomotive where the
controls were explained to them, and they made tape
recordings of the engine, the noise of a porter's barrow, some
chicks waiting in boxes to be loaded on the next train, the
guard's whistle and so on. These were for later use back in
school. All the station staff were very helpful and the
stationmaster had even put on his best uniform in honour of
the visit.

Where a farm is accessible a visit can be most stimulating.
The children examine the machinery, smell and feel straw
and grain, visit the animals and timidly stroke them (perhaps
the first time they have actually seen or touched a live animal
other than a pet dog, cat or bird). The farmer tells them very
simply about his work and shows how the cattle are milked,
then how the milk is treated. On visits like this it is often the
unexpected that has the greatest impact on the children. I
once took some five-, six- and seven-year-olds to a farm.
Towards the end of the visit it was time for milking and the
children were allowed to watch from a raised gallery. All the
visitors, including me, were amazed at the heat that half a
dozen cows generated. The second unexpected highlight of
this visit was a baby fox one of the farmworkers had caught
that the children could stroke. (Did *you* know that baby foxes
have green eyes? Fifteen young children and two adults do —
now).

After such a visit there are many opportunities to talk
about it in school. Stories can be read, and some children will
be seen playing at the activity in the playground. The teacher
should write a 'thank you' letter and read it out for all the

children to hear. If a child has tried to paint a picture of what
has been seen, or has made a collage of it, it may be possible
to send it as a 'present' to the workmen. In this way the
informal use of our surroundings can provide several valuable
educational experiences: the children learn something about
the world, they meet and talk to a wider range of adults, they
gain new ideas and words to go with them, and they learn
something about politeness and courtesy, all in an exciting
but pleasantly informal way.

9 Setting up a playgroup

A teacher who begins working in an established playgroup, or who goes to work in a maintained school (that is one controlled and financed by the Local Education Authority, often wrongly called a state school), is often very fortunate. The organisational and financial problems are taken care of by someone else. The teacher can get on with the job for which she was trained. In addition any class or group already in existence has built up its own momentum; the children already know a lot of what is expected of them. Most of them accept being away from home and are well on the way to becoming socialised. But the playgroup leader or parent who is starting from scratch is in a very different position. There may be months of hard work before the first child is ever admitted, and *by law* this work *must* be done before any child sets foot over the threshold of the school playground or the adults involved may find themselves in serious trouble. Then there are the many problems of raising money to start the group off, and not only to start it but to keep it going, year in, year out. Finally, when this has been achieved, when premises have been found, money raised, equipment purchased, made or renovated, all the legal requirements satisfied, there is the problem of welding ten, twenty or even more children who may never before have been away from home into a happy, hardworking and playing unit; and all this lies against a background of uncertainty on the part of the leader, who very probably is not a trained teacher; or who, if she is trained, is not likely to be experienced in administration and organisation.

However, lest any reader feels put off by this, let us be more positive. The initial work and planning is formidable, but it is not completely impossible. Many of the legal requirements are there to protect our children. For them only the best is good enough. There are many people willing to help with advice, but like the rest of us they are human and busy and will respond better to a polite request from a responsible person who can be seen to be genuinely concerned with trying to solve a serious problem than someone who makes aggressive demands. Unfortunately some people, for various reasons, *do* behave aggressively. This must be avoided at all costs. There are also a number of organisations specifically set up to help parents and playgroup leaders to solve these problems, and the fact that large numbers of playgroups exist, and more are opened every year, should give encouragement.

Proper organisation has its own rewards: people know clearly and in advance what they are supposed to be doing, things are done in the right order and necessary equipment turns up in the right place at the right time. But organisation has other advantages as well. Officials are used to dealing with formal situations and properly constituted bodies. The happy, and perhaps rather 'scatty' amateur who dislikes red tape and tries to cut corners may occasionally be surprisingly successful, but administrators are more likely to help solve problems, to make grants of money and to supply cheap second-hand furniture to an organisation that is run systematically and along recognised lines.

There are also two other great factors that must be considered. In the first place the initial push towards the setting up of a playgroup may come from a group of mothers who perhaps live near to each other. They talk about the needs of their children and discover that one of them is a trained teacher. What is more natural than that she should become a leading light in the movement to set up a playgroup? This can be most useful, but may also be fraught with potential difficulties. If the group is built around one person then if that person disappears the group may disintegrate. The common reason for the disappearance of the central figure is that her own children grow up: few children spend more than two years in a playgroup, and with an average family of two children this may mean that a mother is involved with children of this playgroup age for only four or five years. When her children go on to full-time education, the teacher-mother may wish to return to full-time teaching herself. Another common reason is to be found in the mobility of young families: husbands are promoted and may have to leave the place where they have made their homes. Naturally they take their families with them. Proper organisation achieves continuity. Even if these problems are overcome, it is unreasonable to expect the person who is involved with the education of a group of children to spend a lot of time in administration, public relations, fund-raising and so on. The heads of LEA schools do devote a lot of time to these activities, but they do not usually have a heavy teaching load. Few playgroups are likely to be able to afford a non-teaching leader.

The conclusions are inescapable: any playgroup must be organised formally and this implies the setting up of a properly constituted committee. Once a group of parents has decided to try to set up a playgroup the first step is to form a committee. If they already have in mind one of their own number to be leader, then it is natural that she should be a member of the committee, especially if she is a trained and experienced teacher, but a point to note is that if the group is to be registered as a charity then no one who is employed and paid by the charity may be a voting member of any committee of management, although she may attend meetings.

Apart from the teaching expert, other committee members should, as far as possible, be experienced in the work they will have to do. A local business or professional man may make a very good *chairman*. He probably already knows a lot about running meetings, he has many contacts locally at both business and administrative levels, and so on. His main function is to hold the group together, to mobilise help from outside and to see that the committee is properly run.

An experienced *secretary* is needed to maintain the necessary records of the group and its committee, to prepare reports and agendas and keep minutes, answer letters, and see that new parents are fully briefed about the group and its social functions. It is often useful to have a secretary who knows something of business organisation, who can type or has access to a typist, who realises the importance of keeping records properly and can maintain a proper filing system (every communication inwards and outwards must be safely and systematically filed for reference). There may be need too for someone, either the secretary or a part-time mum, to attend the school on one or two mornings a week to keep track of the daily problems, to deal with queries, to meet visitors when the leader is busy with her children and so on.

The third principal committee member is the *treasurer*. His function is in the first place to maintain a systematic set of accounts. This is not difficult, but it is always useful to have someone who is acquainted with problems of income tax and national insurance contributions. The treasurer will also keep track of all monies received and paid out, and it is best for these to be paid automatically through a bank. Any tendency to think along the lines of, 'Last week I put two quid into petty cash. This one pound fifty will repay me, then the other fifty can come from Mrs Smith's three pounds, so that means I'll only pay two-fifty of her money into the bank today' must be avoided. Memory is fickle and it is very easy to lose track of individual transactions. This may result in parents being asked to pay twice over, which annoys them, or in bills being forgotten, which is bad public relations for the playgroup. All large payments must be considered and authorised by the committee and at least two signatures are usually needed on each cheque paid out. Of course there is always a need for small sums of money to cover day-to-day running expenses. The leader should have at her disposal a sizable petty cash fund that can be replenished as it runs out. Of course she will keep a simple account of how this money is spent, but it is probably not appropriate for this to be under too tight control of the committee: if the leader is responsible enough to be trusted with our children, then she is responsible enough to be trusted with five pounds of petty cash. Accounts must be audited annually and when applications are made for grants or other financial assistance it is normal practice to be asked to submit copies of properly audited accounts, so great and meticulous care is needed in keeping them.

It is often advantageous to have at least one other principal committee member, although a title is often difficult to find for him. His functions are manifold. For example he may be the one who makes sure that news of the playgroup finds its way from time to time into the local press, or he may be the person who ensures that important local people are aware of the aims and achievements of the playgroup. This can best be done by someone who is good at public relations and who can make and keep contracts with local council members, clergymen, Rotary and Inner Wheel organisations and so on. He may also have the function of arranging social and fund-raising activities, although as the playgroup grows it may be better to appoint a separate committee or even sub-committee for this purpose.

Finally it is always useful to keep parents as closely involved as possible with the background running of the playgroup. In part this can be achieved by a regularly appearing newsletter (which may also be displayed on a notice-board in the local library, so that newcomers to the district or to the ranks of parents become aware of the existence of the playgroup), by regular parent-teacher meetings which are used to explain the aims of the group and of modern education to the parents as well as to answer some of their problems and allow them to meet other parents. It is often useful to invite the area psychologist to come and answer parents' questions, or to ask the local adviser for nursery education or someone from the nearest college of education to talk about modern education. In this case it is usual to offer to pay the speaker's travelling expenses and perhaps provide a snack in a member's home.

In addition to these committee members it is useful to get the parents to elect a couple of representatives to the committee. The other committee members may not have children in the group and if this is so it is essential to have some members who are directly involved as 'customers'. I myself am a governor of two primary schools whose governing body must, by regulation, include a number of parent-members. Although they may not be very hot on administration or organisation and may not know too much about the theory and psychology of modern education, their enthusiasm and common sense are of immense benefit. They can mobilise considerable support at short notice when some activity needs a lot of helpers, because they meet other parents daily as they bring their children to school and collect them at hometime. It is often these committee members who can give most help and encouragement to parents new to the district or to the playgroup.

It must be emphasized that the functions of the committee do not include the educational running of the group, although the leader will, if she is wise, keep its members fully informed of what she is doing and may often wish to ask their advice. The function of the committee is to free the leader and her helpers from worries other than the professional ones. This function can be summarised briefly under the following heads:

1 To register the group and to ensure that all legal requirements are met.

2 To find suitable premises and negotiate their use. Where no playgroup exists in the district there may be some prejudice to overcome. Elderly neighbours may be worried about possible noise and trespassing by youthful vandals. The managers of the church hall may fear that the freedom of 'modern education' will result in the floor, destined for next Saturday's dance, being covered with a sticky mixture of sand, clay and poster paints. Each of these doubts must be cleared up, and this is often best done by someone experienced in negotiating, especially if he holds a respected and responsible position locally.

3 Propaganda with local government committees and other important people and organisations. It is useful to keep local councillors informed of the aims of modern pre-school education, to invite them to meet parents, and to visit the playgroup when it is working. In this way the group is likely to gain valuable support. The committees that are likely to be involved in decisions concerning the playgroup are the general purposes, finance, social services and education committee. The town clerk should also be approached for help especially over the best time to apply for grants. He will know when the estimates for the following year are to be discussed. If an application is made after this time then a whole year will elapse before it can be considered.

Among other local organisations that may be useful are the

library, the Rotarians and Inner Wheel, scout and guide companies, charitable trusts and foundations, colleges of education and primary school heads. Some of these will have access to money or materials (furniture, books, etc.) while others may be able to help with temporary part-time helpers. Especially useful here are the guides (working for their child-care badges) and colleges of education, many of whose students enjoy putting in extra work with young children. This may be especially important if the playgroup includes a number of handicapped or socially disadvantaged children. Senior scouts can usually be relied upon to do odd jobs if they are asked, cheerfully undertaking the task of collecting and repairing old toys for the playgroup, mending and repairing furniture and so on. Many secondary schools arrange mothercraft and housecraft courses for their senior pupils and are usually very glad to find somewhere 'real' for them to gain practical experience. The benefits from educating future mothers should not be underrated.

4   To raise money and collect furniture and other equipment. Many wood yards, do-it-yourself shops and builders will allow playgroups to take away off-cuts and sawdust, while paper and card can be obtained from paper mills if there are any locally. It is often easier for committee members to obtain these things and to arrange for them to be collected, and it is not reasonable to expect a leader to give up her Saturdays to act as a general carter to the group. The committee also decides the size of the fees payable per session and the major items of expenditure (in this case after consulting with the leader).

5   A major function of the committee is to appoint staff. If a leader leaves then it is the committee's job to secure another, perhaps arranging for her to receive some training beforehand. Helpers should also be approved by the committee, in consultation with the leader. Problems are usually few but the welfare of the children must be paramount and any helper who appears to have any personality defect should not be allowed near the children however willing she or he may be.

Registering the playgroup

As soon as a committee has been formed and it has been decided who will run it, where it will meet and the likely numbers of children involved, the long process of registration begins. The first step is to write to the local director of social services. His address can be obtained from the local library, citizen's advice bureau or town hall. The initial letter should be quite short and direct, stating the intention to start a playgroup and asking for advice and help. This advice may consist of duplicated or printed details of requirements or involve a visit from a local adviser to discuss the problems, talk about local facilities and possible help. Forms will also be sent, since under the 1968 Health Service and Public Health Act (section 60) any person who cares for a child (who is not a relative) for more than two hours daily for reward must register with the local social services department.

At the same time it would be advisable to register the playgroup with the Pre-school Playgroups Association, the Save the Children Fund or the Nursery School Association (addresses are in the Appendix), each of whom will give fuller details about the setting up and running of playgroups than is possible in this book. They also give advice about insurance, applying for grants and so on.

Suitable premises will probably have been found before this stage and negotiation about their use and any possible alterations for use by young children should have been completed. It usually surprises adults to realise how much of our world is planned around big people. A three-year-old who cannot reach the WC at home may use a potty: imagination boggles at twenty of them doing it! Washbasins, towels, coathooks and many other everyday bits and pieces must be thought of in Lilliputian terms if the premises are to be regarded as suitable for occupation by the very young.

Before putting the social services department to the trouble of inspecting the premises it is as well to check whether planning permission is needed from the town planning committee to use them for business purposes. If it is a church hall used for dances and whist-drives this will probably be a mere formality, but where a private house is involved it becomes more serious as the building is changing its *use*. Opposition from neighbours may result in permission being refused, so it is as well to make sure that the neighbours are in sympathy with the aims of the playgroup. Provision of toilet facilities will be considered, as will emergency exits, access along existing roads (fifty cars a day drawing up in a small cul-de-sac at 9.30, 12.30, 1.30 and 3.30 can cause problems for residents and tradespeople) and many other points. The town planning department will usually give advice and help where necessary, but they may require some alterations to be made before planning permission is given.

Finally the social services department will send along an inspector. Standards of inspection vary from place to place but the aim will be to see that the children involved are cared for properly, that fire precautions are adequate (the local fire brigade will help here with advice) and that the adults will themselves have proper facilities. The inspector will probably set a limit to the number of children who may attend at any one time. This number must not be exceeded. The adults working in the playgroup will need to be examined medically, especially for tuberculosis. This can be done free at mobile clinics (details are usually available in the local library) or may be carried out at a hospital.

Once approval has been given by the director of social services the playgroup is legally able to begin operations but there are many other problems to be solved before the first child enters.

Thus under the Welfare Food Act of 1968, children are entitled to receive a third of a pint of milk daily. This must be paid for and reimbursement sought later. Application forms (WF/DN15A) must be obtained from:

The Department of Health and Social Security
Alexander Fleming House
Elephant and Castle
London SE1

The form must be completed by the playgroup and sent to the local director of social services for certification. He will return it to the playgroup and it must be sent immediately to the DHSS. Form WF/DN 16 will be returned by the DHSS, and this enables money to be claimed back if it is accompanied by receipts from the dairy that supplies the milk together with a record of the children's attendance.

Playgroups in Scotland must apply to the Scottish Home and Health Group,

12—14 Carlton Terrace
Edinburgh EH7 5DG

The form will then be sent to the local director of social work for countersigning. Otherwise the procedure is the same as in England. It should be noted that no reimbursement can be made for milk supplied before registration, which is held to be effective either from the date of the first letter or the date on which milk is first supplied, whichever is the later.

In place of or in addition to milk it may be desired to give orange juice. This is not free but may be obtained by a properly registered playgroup from the local health officials.

Registration as a charity

When a playgroup is formed serious thought must be given to its legal status, since this involves, among other things, the way its income is taxed. Few playgroups are run as businesses, making a profit for the leader, but where this is the case advice should be sought from an accountant about claiming full expenses. Most playgroups are organised either as non-profit-making organisations or as charities. The difficulty with the former is that your views on whether extra funds are to be seen as profits or as balancing surpluses (a profit from one year that offsets a loss the next) may differ depending on whether you are a playgroup committee member or the local inspector of taxes. Most inspectors are sympathetic and humane people who will listen to a reasoned case, but need for this can be avoided if the playgroup is registered as a charity. Charities are exempt from paying income tax and are eligible for grants from other charities. They fall into a recognised legal category (and this makes the task of administrators easier) and generally receive more sympathy from local government officials and the public. In fact most playgroups will *not* need to register, being specifically exempt from this under the 1960 Charities Act. It is as well to apply to the Charity Commissioners:

The Charity Commissioners for England and Wales
14 Ryder Street
St James's
London SW17 6AH
for information and for the registration form RE 1. This
form must be returned to the Charity Commissioners
together with the playgroup's constitution, certificated by
the group's officers. The date of adoption of the constitution
must be shown. In Scotland playgroups should apply to their
local Inland Revenue Department. In some cases the
Commissioners may require certain changes to be made in the
constitution. This can cause delay and to avoid this a
standard form of constitution should be used, like that
available from the Pre-school Playgroups Association. It is
probable that the playgroup will be registered as a 'charity
not required to register'. With these words the playgroup
acquires charitable status.

It is important that this should be done *before* any fees are
received, as soon as a constitution has been adopted,
otherwise some tax may have to be paid on money received
before this time. The local Inland Revenue office should.be
contacted at an early date, and exemption can be claimed
from the Inland Revenue Department, if in Scotland or (for
groups in England and Wales) from:
The Chief Inspector of Taxes (Claims)
Magdalen House
Stanley Precinct
Bootle, Lancashire L69 9BB

The constitution
The constitution should be a clear statement of the aims of
the playgroup and rules by which it is to be conducted.
Model copies can be obtained from the Pre-school Playgroup
Association, but where committees decide to write their own
constitution it should be sent for approval (and probable
alteration) to:
The Department of Education and Science
Curzon Street
London W1

Insurance
Playgroups are likely to involve two sorts of insurance, *which must not be confused.*

In the first place they must pay national insurance contributions on all employees. How much has to be paid depends on the nature of the employment (especially hours of work and earnings) and upon the employee's personal circumstances. Details may be obtained from the local Department of Health and Social Security.

In a very different category is insurance for legal liability for any accidents that may happen. The playgroup leader's liability to young children with a long life expectancy will be particularly high. The group is also liable for accidents to employees. Where apparatus and equipment is involved it may be necessary to insure this too against theft and fire. In some cases playgroups may be already covered by existing policies taken out to cover use of, say, a parish hall. However, careful enquiry must be made, especially as this insurance is probably aimed at adult, or at most adolescent, use. In no case should it be assumed that insurance cover exists or is adequate. Different insurance companies offer different sorts of cover and make different charges. It is useful to adopt a standard form of insurance, such as that recommended by the Pre-school Playgroup Association.

Contracts of Employment
Under the Contracts of Employment Act of 1963 employers must give their employees a written statement outlining the main terms of their employment. This includes references to pay, hours of work, duties, holidays, any pension rights, period of notice required on both sides, etcetera. Such a contract is legally necessary only for employees who work more than twenty-one hours a week. In a playgroup with one full-time leader and several part-time helpers, it is probably only the leader who needs the contract as a legal require-ment. However, in the interests of fostering a professional attitude to the work it may be desirable to give part-time helpers a contract if their help is regular, say, every morning or afternoon. Apart from the question of courtesy, there is a good psychological reason for this practice: it emphasises the

serious nature of the undertaking. Agreement to help should neither be accepted nor laid down lightly. It also raises the status of what may appear to some people to be a rather lowly job.

Where help is given freely by mothers on a rota basis, it is also well to present every mother with a similar document although as no payment is involved it has no legal standing as a contract. If aims are spelled out, authority clearly demonstrated, and some formal recognition of the times and dates of such help are given, mothers will be impressed by the businesslike arrangements. It is not unknown for a mother to agree to help, but to forget her commitment later when some emergency occurs or the sales are on. A subsidiary benefit is that some mothers, as a result of their experience in helping in a playgroup, may decide they would like to train to teach. Many of them may spend several years obtaining GCE passes at evening school or through correspondence courses. Some official document that gives evidence of what they have been doing and over what period may help them to secure a place on a teacher training course at a college of education.

A problem sometimes arises in playgroups over the fees of children from poorer homes. It may be that the committee feel that some socially disadvantaged children would benefit from attendance at the playgroup. However if their parents cannot pay the fees (which may come to a pound or more for a half-day, five times a week) and if the playgroup's finances cannot bear the strain of non-paying members, then some alternative arrangement must be made. Sometimes these children are allowed to attend free, and the mothers do some necessary work in payment. This is probably unwise as it smacks of charity, and people have their pride. In addition what comes free is often undervalued. If a mother works then it might be better in this case to pay her a reasonable wage so that she can, in turn, pay for her child to attend. In any case every playgroup should overbudget to some extent. It may be that through illness or unemployment a family falls on hard times. Where this happens it would be inhumane to exclude a child who could not pay his fees. However, any form of financial help that is given should be offered in private, if possible only the chairman, treasurer and leader knowing anything of the matter.

Financing the playgroup
There are several different sources of finance available, but
most playgroups will have to raise some money for themselves, at least initially. Grants may be received from local
authorities, but they are not mandatory, and playgroup
committees must prepare and present a case that will stand
up to public scrutiny. Applications must also be made at the
right time in the financial year so that grants may be included
in the estimates for the following twelve months. Playgroups
must remember that they are merely one organisation among
many competing for a slice of a cake that may be severely
limited in size. This also applies to appeals for assistance from
charitable trusts and foundations.

In general most local authorities are sympathetic to
appeals for help for playgroups, and over recent years there
has been a steady increase in the numbers and sizes of grants
awarded. In 1973 a little over forty per cent of playgroups
received hundred per cent grants, while another eight per
cent received seventy-five per cent. On the other hand twenty
per cent (that is, one out of every five playgroups) received
no help at all. We see therefore that some at least of the
necessary money will have to be raised by the playgroup
itself. It may be that in the first year or two all the costs,
both of initial outlay and running costs, will have to be
found, until the group has established its *bona fides* and
convinced local people not only that its aims are sound but
that a group of responsible people is prepared to do
something for itself in order to achieve these aims. In some
ways local authorities are like God: they help those who help
themselves.

First let us consider what sort of money is likely to be
needed to set up and run a playgroup. Undoubtedly the
largest item will be salaries. The required ratio of adults to
children in nursery groups is one to eight. Thus with
twenty-four children, which is probably the limit for one
class although playgroups may eventually include two or
three such classes, one trained leader and two assistants are
needed. It is possible and indeed desirable to involve parents

in the day-to-day running of the group. We must remember that groups should not be seen as replacing parents so much as supplementing them. Mothers (and fathers too if they are free and willing) may take their places in a rota, coming in to help one half-day a week or fortnight, depending on the number who are willing and able to share. But it is desirable to have, in addition to the leader, at least one salaried assistant. It may be that the leader falls ill or encounters some emergency at home, and if this happens it is unreasonable to expect a mother who is untrained and inexperienced and who normally comes to help only two or three times a term, suddenly to have to cope with twenty-four lively youngsters. Many parents would probably have serious misgivings about the welfare of their children if this were to happen often. But an assistant, whose commitment is seen as extensive, who is there all the time and who may have been trained by the leader, can step in at a moment's notice. She will have met a wider circle of other parents and may be able, after judicious telephoning, to arrange for other mothers to come in and help even at short notice. In addition a salaried assistant might reasonably be expected and encouraged to seek qualifications, possibly by attendance at part-time courses, in order to improve her own skills. Finally, if the leader should have to leave the playgroup, her assistant may be in a position to replace her, thus ensuring continuity.

Let us assume then, that we have a leader and one assistant working full-time (that is, two sessions daily). In addition there will be parents taking turns to help, but they are not normally paid.

Salaried staff may be employed on either an 'all-year-round' basis or a 'termly' basis, and they may receive a fixed salary, calculated on a yearly basis and paid in twelve equal monthly instalments, or they may be paid on a 'time-rate' basis, according to the number of hours they actually spend on the job. It is probable that, in the long run, there will be very little difference between the total amount of money to be found under either system. 'All-year-round' staff normally run the playgroup throughout the year, including school holidays. They receive four weeks' paid holiday each year, together with the usual public holidays. 'Termly' staff work during normal LEA terms only. In this case the playgroup closes during the normal school holidays. When it is planned to set up a playgroup a decision must be made in advance as to which arrangement best suits local conditions. Where many mothers work then an 'all-year-round' system is likely to be best.

The Save the Children Fund make up to date recommendations about adequate current rates of pay. Interested readers should write to them for details, but it is probable that, at present, something in the region of £1,000 each year will have to be found for a full-time, all-year-round leader. Leaders on a termly rate and assistants earn rather less. Hours of work are normally 9 am to 4 pm Mondays to Fridays. This time includes one hour for lunch and thirty minutes at the beginning and end of the day preparing materials and clearing up the classroom or playroom. Some parents may need to leave their children earlier and in some playgroups the staff are present at 8.30, or even 8 am. If this is necessary then payment should be made for the additional work involved.

Other Staff
It may be thought useful to employ a cleaner to help at the end of the day and a 'tea lady' to make mid-morning coffee, sort out the children's milk (and perhaps warm it slightly in winter), help with lunches (if supplied) and so on. These helpers will receive rates of payment current in the locality. Alternatively parents may agree to take it in turn to perform these tasks.

Children usually attend for only half a day, the morning session lasting two and a half hours, the afternoon two. In this case there is no need to provide lunches; it may be necessary for a minority, but it should be avoided wherever possible. These children will normally have a rest after lunch and their nap may be disturbed by the arrival of the afternoon children. In addition kitchen space will be necessary, together with additional furniture for dining. In spite of this, meals can become a useful source of social training: eating quietly after washing hands, passing things politely and so on. Many children bring a snack for elevenses, but some children may not bring any food with them and in this case the school may provide a biscuit or piece of fruit. There is much to be said for providing this in any case: parents often give their children sweets and sticky buns to the detriment of their teeth. If food is provided it must be allowed for in the budget.

Capital outlay
(a) Premises   Money must be available for various purposes even before the playgroup is registered. The premises may need modification. If a private house is involved then the areas designated for the playgroup may need to be clearly marked off from the private quarters. It may be that a door needs to be built to prevent wandering by the inquisitive young. The planning authority may decide that fences need to be renewed, a wall or secure gates provided. Almost certainly the plumbing will need some modification: low-level WCs, washbasins, towel and coat racks are essential. This may not be possible in a public hall, in which case wooden boxes and stands are needed so that the children can reach adult-sized WCs and wash-basins. Some form of safe central heating may need to be installed and where necessary fireguards provided and securely fixed. Groups may be required to provide a proper supply of fire extinguishers, and to modify or increase the number of emergency exits.
(b) Playgroup equipment etc.   Playgroups will undoubtedly begin with only a limited amount of equipment and gradually build up their provision over the early years. However, some things are essential and should be provided from the beginning. This essential equipment should include:
    water tray
    sand tray
    set of nesting boxes
    storage cupboards (on wheels if the material has to be stored daily)
    screens or bookshelves (also on wheels if necessary)
In addition there will be a minimum number of toys, books, sheets of paper, paints, chalks, crayons, paste, flour and sand. A set of small, nursery furniture is essential, including two or three low tables, and at least one low chair per child while adult helpers and visitors all need full-sized chairs, and each

room should also contain one full-sized table or desk in which things can be locked away. Some of these, such as the table or desk, may not be possible, especially if a church hall is used and all equipment must be cleared away each day in order to leave the hall ready for other users. In this case nothing should be left out. Although the scouts local dramatic society and others who use the premises will complain vociferously if *their* property is damaged, it never seems to make them more careful with that of others. This is a strange aspect of human nature for which there is no convincing explanation.

Later, as the playgroup funds increase, it may be possible to provide a sand-pit in a covered space out of doors and a fixed climbing frame. Where public premises are used permission for these to be installed must first be sought from the owners. They must also be robust enough to support the weight of some large senior scouts or even adult swinging on them, and any damage will probably have to be accepted philosophically.

Some playgroups may be sited near a park or recreation ground with its children's section. If so, there is less need for the swings, see-saw, climbing frames and roundabouts to be installed. Regular visits can be made to the public playgrounds when the weather is suitable. Here, though, care is needed: other children will be using these facilities and any tendency to view them as 'ours because we always use them' must be resisted in the interests of good public relations.

When a playgroup is being set up it is as well to enquire of the local education offices whether they have any old nursery and infant school furniture available. With luck they will be renewing the stock in one of their schools and will be willing to sell the old furniture cheaply. It may need some attention, but in this case it is possible to mobilise a group of fathers one weekend. Supply them with glasspaper, paint and varnish and within a very short time the furniture will be as good as new.

(c) Office equipment   Since the playgroup is to be run as a serious concern, the committee should decide to be as businesslike as possible from the beginning. There should be an office, with proper furniture and equipment. If this can be

set up in a separate room, all well and good, but it may have to occupy one corner of the main playroom. Where a church hall is being used there may be a committee room available and the use of this should be negotiated. In this case it is probable that there will already be a table, chairs and telephone, but the playgroup should at least have its own filing cabinet. There are certain records that must be kept by law, and others that are desirable, and these may well be of a confidential nature. Let us assume that we are in the happy position of having a small room available for sole use of the playgroup. What then is needed? At the very least there must be a table and chairs (at least two, one for the leader and one for visiting mothers; three are better, then visiting fathers can be seated as well). There must also be some form of heating, a filing cabinet and telephone. The telephone is essential today and where one cannot be fitted for sole use of the playgroup then unambiguous arrangements for the use of an existing phone must be made before the playgroup begins to operate. If possible a typewriter should be available and, although this is probably to be classed as a luxury, some form of duplicator. As with the other equipment, some of this office furniture may be available second hand. Local businesses can be approached for old office equipment, and the commerce departments of colleges of further education often renew their machines fairly frequently.

It should be a long-term aim of the committee to provide one other room, although for most playgroups this is probably impossible. This will be used for staff members to have their cups of tea, for the local child guidance psychologist to examine children if he visits the playgroup, and for children who feel unwell to rest in. This room will require some comfortable chairs, a point for an electric kettle, a table and a first-aid kit.

In addition to this large-scale equipment, the playgroup will need a supply of minor materials — stamps, paper for letters (perhaps headed; the cost is comparatively cheap, the effect great), paper for duplicating circulars to parents, record books and so on. An initial supply is essential, although it will have to be replenished as time goes on.

Running costs

The materials used by the children — paints, paste, crayons and paper — will have to be constantly renewed. It is difficult to cost these in advance but advice may be given by the local education offices. Groups should try to make *at least* the same provision as would be found in a maintained nursery school (that is, one controlled by a local education authority).

One must also budget for repairs to major items of equipment. In the early years this should not amount to much, in which case the money may be used for buying new items that the group needs and that could not be afforded earlier. These repair costs can be minimised if groups of fathers (or mothers) are organised to keep the furniture smart with glasspaper and paint. Many parents who doubt their ability or confidence to act as an assistant in the group with the actual children may be willing to make a practical contribution in this way. By doing these jobs during the day when the group is in session they may acquire more self-confidence to help in other ways as well.

Other recurring costs that must be met are:

rent
rates
printing
fuel and lighting bills
insurance
national insurance
membership of a national body

It is usual, too, to offer to pay the travelling expenses of staff, committee members or parents who attend courses or meetings in connection with their work in the playgroup. Such payments are often refused, but they should be offered as a courtesy. No one should *unwillingly* be out of pocket as a result of his services to the playgroup.

No attempt has been made to put a figure to any of these items, except for salaries. In a time of inflation the figures rapidly become out of date and can then mislead people. A list of suppliers from whom catalogues can be obtained is given in the Appendix and these should be consulted at an early stage in the process of setting up the playgroup. At current (1974) prices, for a playgroup of forty-eight children, with twenty-four attending the morning session and an equal number in the afternoon, committees should reckon on needing perhaps some £500 to set the group up and between £2,000 and £3,500 (including salaries) to run it. It must be emphasised that these sums include salaries for one full-time leader and one full-time assistant, receiving the current maximum payment. In the early days the lower figure will probably be a more accurate estimate, but eventually the higher sum will have to be found, and allowance made for inflationary increases. It is essential for the playgroup leader to encourage mum-volunteers to come along and help, and she will probably have to train them to carry out her preferred policy. This has two main advantages: costs are kept as low as possible, and (more importantly) the play-group will not be seen as a substitute for the home, but as an extension of it.

Although it would be wise to begin the group in a small way, it is probably more economic to try to increase the numbers as experience is gained: up to fifty children is about the outside limit. For smaller groups fewer staff are needed and this can cut down the running costs, but the structural alterations to premises will be much the same. It is therefore sensible to spread the costs over a greater number of units. Another factor to be considered is that although smaller numbers of children mean fewer staff and smaller amounts of furniture and dispensable material, the income from fees is also less. Again where fewer children are involved it may be more difficult to enlist the occasional help of parents as part-time assistants. Thus, if out of fifty parents forty mothers are willing to help, the commitment of each will be only one half-day every three weeks. Many people may be willing to do this, but with only ten mothers then the turn of each comes up every week, and this may not always be possible.

Raising the money
Where no grant or only a partial grant is available each playgroup will have to raise its own funds. There are many ways of doing this and it is in this sphere that many parents

who feel they could not help with the actual children in the group come into their own. Some parents never seem to run out of bright ideas for raising money, nor, an even more important point, do they flag in their efforts to put their ideas into practice. Any group who is fortunate to possess one such should elect him or coopt him on to their committee: he is too valuable to be lost.

The most straightforward means of raising money is by charging fees. These should be kept as low as possible, since it is no one's intention to exclude less well-off children merely because they cannot afford it. On the other hand the playgroup must be paid for, so it is reasonable to make some charge. Fees tend to vary between 10 and 25p per session (half a day). This means that weekly fees vary between 50p and £1.25. Whatever level the committee decides on in view of other sources of income, new parents must have the arrangements made clear to them. They must know how much they will have to pay, and when and how the payment should be made. Families that hit hard times may be treated generously and with understanding, but otherwise a firm line must be adopted from the beginning: arrears must not be allowed to mount up. The question about payment of fees for missed sessions often arises. As a general rule odd missed sessions should be paid for: the place cannot be filled, the costs continue and the service is there. Of course, if parents give advance notice that they will be away for two or three weeks, this is a different matter, as is absence due to prolonged illness. Most parents accept that payment for odd missed sessions is reasonable, so long as the rule is made clear from the beginning.

One major advantage of the fee system, as opposed to other fund-raising activities, is that the committee can budget ahead: they know roughly how much they can expect to receive. Thus in a playgroup of fifty children 20p per head over a thirty-two week academic year will amount to £1,600. Ten children paying 10p per session will yield only £5 a week, which is probably insufficient to cover costs. In this case fund-raising chores fall heavily on only a few shoulders.

Group activities

There are many old favourites that should not be neglected. The coffee morning may bring in only a pound or two, but a weekly one held in a different home each time can provide thirty or more pounds each year. These functions have another purpose than the purely financial one. As mentioned earlier some parents may be able to contribute to the group in this way rather than in others, and mothers and fathers are enabled to widen their circle of friends and acquaintances. They discover that they are not the only people to have problems with their children. Newcomers to the district may, through meeting other parents, feel less lonely, and this could be important, especially for a young wife and mother whose husband is at work all day and who has left one set of friends behind when she moved to her new home.

Some of the common, well-tried ideas that are always popular are:

coffee mornings
wine and cheese parties
fashion parades
jumble sales or bazaars
garden fêtes
paper collections
bottle and jam jar collections
raffles and draws
dances.

A garden fête needs a large garden, but where one is available it is possible to hire marquees and set up stalls with toys used clothing, books, fruit, cakes, jam, together with bingo and games of skill. It may be possible to get the local scouts to build an aerial ropeway on which rides can be given. Once the large garden has been found, what is most needed is imagination. Thereafter the money flows in. Equally a fashion show needs sizable premises.

Many other ideas are given in the booklet published by the Pre-school Playgroups Association *But Where Does the Money Come From?*, price 12p.

These and other activities that might suggest themselves are not mutually exclusive. There is no reason why any playgroup should not use them all. Coffee mornings can occur throughout the year, while wine and cheese parties come around more rarely — perhaps in spring and autumn. A jumble sale may be arranged at the beginning of the school year or in the spring, while a garden fête is usually most successful in early summer (avoid August which is statistically the wettest month of the year). Raffles and draws usually reach their peak just before Christmas. Collections of waste paper or bottles should be made with an eye to the market. I was once made responsible for collecting waste paper at a time when it was fetching over £18 a ton. Over the weeks more than two tons were collected, but before the paper could be sold the Korean war came to an end and the price fell so low that no one was interested. In the end I got five pounds for the lot in a local fish and chip shop; but I had to carry it there in a rucksack!

One other word of warning is needed: the committee should try to keep its collective ear to the ground locally. To arrange a discothèque on the one evening that a pop group is visiting the nearby town is to court disaster. To arrange the garden fête when the local scouts have theirs, when the county agricultural show is in full swing and when the cricket club dance is to be held the same evening is not likely to swell the funds of the playgroup.

Grants from public funds
Although grants to playgroups from local authorities are permissive and not mandatory, there are many different acts of parliament enabling the authorities to give financial help. When making application for a grant it may be useful to quote these, together with examples of the generosity of other authorities, especially if they are nearby: there is nothing like local rivalry to loosen the purse-strings. Full details can be obtained from the national bodies already mentioned, and particularly useful is the PPA booklet, *Local Authorities and Playgroups*.

Needless to say requests should always be polite, with no hint of demands, and preferably following meetings with councillors who have been told of the aims of the movement as well as the steps that have been taken to meet them. On the whole local authorities are sympathetic to requests for help from responsible groups of citizens trying to do something worthwhile and who are already sacrificing some of their own time and energy.

We have already seen that five out of ten playgroups receive a hundred or seventy-five per cent grants. Another three out of every ten receive sizable grants, and only two out of ten receive no help whatever. Even where a large grant is not forthcoming, local authorities may be able to give not ungenerous help. Thus many of them make an almost automatic foundation grant of twenty to fifty pounds or even more. In some cases help may be given with modifying premises, such as providing low-level lavatories. In one case a Midlands authority granted a loan of £3,500 for a playgroup building on a new estate towards which the parents were contributing £1,000. Where the playgroup opens its doors to a number of children at risk, special help is often given to the group in the form of fees, foundation grants, payment of fees for leaders, assistants attending courses, and other things while it is nearly standard practice for the fees of handicapped children to be paid by the local authority. In this case too one may be sure that very favourable consideration will be given to requests for unwanted furniture. In addition many local authorities allow playgroups to purchase equipment and supplies at cost price through the school supplies service.

Where an authority cannot make a grant of its own it may be able to obtain one through Urban Aid. Such grants and help will depend on the playgroup being properly constituted and run. It should be a member of one of the national bodies, and of course all legal obligations concerned with registration must be fulfilled. The director of education will need to be sure that the activities provided fulfil the social and educational needs of pre-school children and that the staff are fit persons to have the care of young children and are properly qualified. The doors of the playgroup must be open to all children in the neighbourhood (with some form of reasonable selection where demand outstrips provision). Groups will often be asked to include some children at risk because of impoverished background or handicap.

Training for personnel

At least one of the playgroup supervisors must be trained, and she should try to see that her assistants also receive some training. Courses of training vary. There is a one-year full-time course held at

Thurrock Technical College

Grays

Essex

Other training courses leading to the Nursery Nurses Examination Board certificate can be obtained. This is likely to involve a period of full-time training, and as such may not be suitable for the leader of a newly established playgroup who probably has a young family of her own. The Pre-school Playgroups Association organises part-time courses for leaders and assistants, and many local authorities also arrange similar courses, while some colleges of education can give help. Other useful sources of education and training can be reached through other bodies. Thus, for example, if enough interest is shown, the Workers' Educational Association may be able to arrange a series of lectures in child development. These are rather more general than courses specifically designed for leaders of playgroups would be, but many parents are interested in learning more about their children. I have given a number of these courses, arranged at the request of groups of parents. It has frequently happened that both fathers and mothers attended, and a large part of the courses became devoted to the actual problems that the class-members' children were experiencing, with not a few of their own problems being discussed sympathetically and advice given by other members of the class as well as by the tutor. Attendance at such a course may be a useful introduction to rather more specialised training. It may also be possible to get a local college of further education to arrange courses devoted to parent-education. At least one college of further education used to run a two-year course for parents. Part of the course was devoted to child development, while other parts were devoted to some aspects of sociology and parents could, if they wished, prepare to take two or three GCE O-level examinations in order to fit themselves for future courses of teacher training as mature students.

The children

Some information has been given in passing on numbers of children, hours of attendance and so on. When parents begin talking of setting up a playgroup most of them will undoubtedly think first of their own children. This is inevitable, and such a playgroup may provide a valuable service. It is likely, however, to be rather unstable, and once a more permanent organisation is set up then the needs of a wider range of children can be considered. Two classes of children with special needs are likely to come the way of many playgroups, especially if grants are made from public funds. While special attention and sympathy should be given to these children, care must be taken that they do not occupy too many places. The advantage that children with special needs can gain from membership of a playgroup comes from their experiences in mixing with a stable group of happy, normal children. Where the 'special' children equal or outnumber the others then this advantage is lost.

The first group of children with special needs is likely to be those from socially disadvantaged homes. The social difficulties may arise from the lack of money in a broken single-parent family, or from the personal inability of the mother to care properly for her family, which may very likely be oversize as well. Many of these children may present behaviour problems that derive mainly from the inadequate and often conflicting social training and example that they have been exposed to at home. It was such children who were referred to in the Plowden Report (see the Epilogue) as being at risk and it is probably they who will benefit from a stable environment in which positive reinforcement is used to direct their behaviour. Many of these children will be found to have impoverished language skills, to show limited spans of attention, to be unable to concentrate for any time on many activities, to behave selfishly with toys and so on. The lack of success reported in the Plowden Report was probably due to the very freedom that these children encountered in their playgroups. Most children are reinforced (quite unconsciously) at home in the direction of being quiet, caring and sharing with others, and so on. If a child has not had this training at home then he will need it at school. Total freedom merely allows his unwelcome habits to become stronger, and when, as is inevitable, he is reprimanded or punished he will come to see the adult as a hated figure who interferes with his desires. He may learn to hide these when the adult is around, but this does not mean that they have been eradicated. We must be clear that I am not urging harsh, repressive discipline here, but the gentle and judicious shaping of behaviour along desired lines, as discussed earlier.

The other group will consist of handicapped children. The handicaps are likely to be defective eyesight or hearing, other physical handicaps and also mental handicaps, although it is unlikely that playgroups will be asked to take serious cases. Sometimes parents may have misgivings that their children will be 'contaminated' in some way by these handicapped children. This is extremely unlikely. To an increasing extent it is being realised that the strange behaviour that one sometimes observes in handicapped children is due not so much to their handicap as to the treatment they receive as handicapped people. That is if, say, parents are told that their child must not be thwarted in any way lest he has an attack of asthma, or because he has a weak heart, they will form habits of giving in to his every whim. His brothers and sisters will be forced to give way to him, whether he wants to disrupt their games, take their toys, or whatever. It is not uncommon for them to leave home as soon as they can to escape the domination of a child who is turned into a selfish ogre by the treatment he receives. But it is not the handicap that has caused this antisocial behaviour. Handicaps are neutral. It is people who mould behaviour. Experts are coming increasingly to realise that the handicapped child's greatest handicap is not in fact his handicap at all, but the attitudes, habits and expectations that his parents and teachers have of him as a handicapped person. For these children to experience a normal, stable, happy playgroup atmosphere, in which they come to realise they have rights and also obligations, is the only way that they will grow up to be normal adults, who just happen to have a problem of hearing, or heart, or whatever.

Teachers may have misgivings about their ability to teach children with handicaps, especially when they see around them special schools and special training courses each claiming to impart some expertise. Now, there is *some* expertise involved, and playgroup leaders may expect to receive help in this. But again what is needed more than anything is a warm, tolerant atmosphere. The teacher must make sure that the little girl with poor vision, or the boy with the hearing aid sit near her when she tells a story. The intellectually retarded child may need extra explanations before he seems to understand, and he may seem quickly to forget what he has learned. But these problems do not demand genius or special expertise. They need imagination, humanity and some patience.

As regards the special technical problems it is reasonable to expect help from the local educational psychologist. He may be overworked (most counties do not have enough of them) but if he has asked a playgroup to take in one or two children he should be asked to visit the school frequently to see how the children are getting on, to help the leader and her helpers and possibly to demonstrate some important points to them.

Other bodies that may be approached for help and advice include the Royal National Institute for the Deaf, the Royal National Institute for the Blind, the Spastics Society, and many other societies, each devoted to children suffering from a different handicap. A list of useful addresses is given in the Appendix. When a playgroup leader writes to these bodies she should simply explain her problem. The organisations will probably send leaflets and may even be able to put the playgroup in contact with a trained and experienced teacher who lives nearby, or with the nearest school for that handicap. It may be possible to arrange for a visitor to come to the school to talk about the problem and ways of dealing with it. Sometimes films are available and these can be usefully linked with a fund-raising coffee evening in order to help parents to understand the needs of these children.

Local education authorities will also be interested. Each has advisers who will be able to make useful suggestions. Increasingly, too, counties are employing peripatetic teachers of the deaf, whose function is to work with hearing-handicapped children who are in normal schools, to advise and train parents to help their children and to give help to ordinary teachers where necessary. They are usually very busy and have large caseloads but will often try to fit a regular visit to a playgroup into the schedules.

Records

We have already seen that it is essential to maintain proper financial records of the playgroup. There are others no less essential. Some of these are prescribed by law and must include:

(a) each child's name, address and home telephone number (if there is one);

(b) the date of birth;

(c) the mother's place of work and telephone number;

(d) the name of the family doctor, his address and telephone number.

In addition a daily attendance register must be kept. There are also other items that the playgroup leader should know. It may be that a child does not have a telephone at home. In this case it may be possible to obtain the number of a neighbour who would be willing to carry a message in case of emergency. The parents must be asked to arrange this. Again, it may be that the child needs to go home a little early on some occasions. Needless to say no child should be allowed to leave the group on his own earlier than his parents expect or than is usual. If this should happen and the child is injured the playgroup and its leader will probably be liable to heavy damages at law. If a child must leave early he must be taken by the leader or other responsible adult, and it is as well to know whether one of the neighbours would be prepared to take the child in, in case the mother has just 'popped out to the shops'.

There is also some useful medical information that playgroups should possess on their records. These include a record of inocculations and other immunisations, including tetanus protection. Physical weaknesses should be noted so that care can be taken of the child and any allergies should also be recorded. I know of one tragic case where a boy was given a penicillin injection after a comparatively slight accident. He was allergic to penicillin and became very ill, as a result of which he totally lost his hearing.

Some teachers attempt to keep full records of IQ, attainment (often assessed by the teacher) and so on where they are available. The reasoning behind this seems to be that a proper set of records looks somehow 'more scientific' and that, if the teacher changes, then continuity of treatment will be achieved. There is something (but not much — see below) to be said for the latter of these reasons, but nothing whatever in support of the former. Scientific records are as strong or weak as the data on which they are based, and most IQ, attainment and personality estimates have very little value, even when made by a trained psychologist. Made by an amateur they are not worth the paper they are written on. In addition they have a serious drawback. We know that something of the assessor enters into every assessment. Some people are optimistic and take a sunny view of others, while their colleagues are far more pessimistic. Some teachers value children who talk frequently, others suspect them of being 'smart alecs'. It is well known that all teachers tend to over-evaluate middle-class children (who come from homes similar to the teachers'), whose parents probably read the same kinds of newspaper and watch the same sorts of television programmes while they under-evaluate many working-class children, especially if they speak badly, or are a bit 'agin the school'. In short, teachers (and probably everyone else!) tend to over-estimate the intelligence of people who resemble them and under-estimate those who do not.

Even this would not be too bad, but we are becoming increasingly aware of a phenomenon known as 'teacher expectations'. A lot of results suggest that, even if she does nothing special about it, if a teacher believes that a child is potentially a high flyer, then within a very short space of time that child begins to improve his performance. On the other hand a child who is believed to have low potential tends gradually to justify this belief. The reason is probably to be found in all sorts of interpersonal reactions that may be difficult to detect. When a teacher believes that a child has potential, she probably pays him a little more attention, smiles at his comments, accepts errors as 'slips of the tongue' and so on. A positive reinforcing situation is set up. Since this makes the child feel good he will tend to try to repeat the behaviour which has achieved this desirable end in the past. But for his classmate who is more poorly evaluated, who is believed to have less potential, things are very different. Without realising it the teacher pays less attention: her smiles may be less frequent, she listens with only half an ear. Any bright comments that may be right are passed off as 'flashes' or attempts to 'take the micky' and so on. The child may be less frequently asked to do the prized classroom chores like putting straws in the milk bottles, helping with the chairs and so on. His reinforcement is in a very different direction.

This 'teacher expectation' phenomenon has been demonstrated in many different settings, with handicapped and non-handicapped children, with children from richer homes and those from poorer, and so on. It must be stressed that no one in the situations described was conscious of what he was doing. There is more to communication than words. Every time we speak we signal to our hearers more than merely the message we consciously intend to give. The way we stand, our tone of voice, the words we use, the way we listen to the reply, all of these signal to the other person what we think about him. Because we are unconscious of what we are doing we cannot often prevent this. An example we have probably all participated in is the sort of argument that sometimes arises between husband and wife, or friends or colleagues:

'But I only said . . . '

'You might have *only said* that, but you really meant . . . '

The lesson for us in this is to beware of records made by other people. They might be 'right' or they might be 'wrong'. Whatever they are they will contain something of the other person in them. If we read them then our approach to the child is already conditioned in one way or another: 'Mary is a good girl, but John is a trouble-maker, watch him.' We are almost certain to find that Mary and John both live up to their reputations. If they don't we might be worried that we are wrong! More likely we will believe that they have both changed. Neither is true. Mary *was* good in response to your predecessor in the situations she created. She *may* be good in response to you and in the situations you create. She may not. It is better to work it out for yourself from first principles.

If any records are kept they should be merely *aides mémoires* to the teachers. When a child gives evidence of readiness to move on to some new skill or activity then it is useful to note this down somewhere. Many teachers keep records like this 'in their heads' but with twenty-five or so children developing separately and rapidly this is difficult. If records such as those suggested are kept, then the teacher can look back at the end of every term. If she finds that only a few children are mentioned then it may be that the leader has formed the habit of judging the success of her group on the basis of only a small number of 'high flyers'. For the rest of the children the group may be failing in its aims, and the teacher or leader may not even realise it. Perhaps even more serious is the case where a child is not mentioned at all. He may have made progress or he may not. Certainly he has been neglected by the leader, and something should be done at once to remedy this sad state of affairs. The success or failure of any educational institution must be judged on the effects it has had on *all* its pupils, not on the striking and acceptable behaviour of a small handful alone.

Another useful record is the log book — a sort of diary, with photographs, pressed flowers and leaves, recording exciting trips, visitors and so on.

Premises and apparatus

Most playgroups will not be well endowed. At least at the beginning they will have to put up with less than ideal conditions in premises and equipment. Gradually the apparatus will accumulate, much of it probably home-made. This is not necessarily a bad thing. It may seem to be a fatiguing chore to have to build your own set of bookshelves, but at least they will fit your premises. It is surprising how often some piece of expensive apparatus or furniture isn't *quite* what we want, doesn't *quite* fit the place where we want to put it and so on. There is no excuse for this when the furniture is home-made, except carelessness and lack of skill (always points to be borne in mind when amateurs are involved!). No great skill is needed, although the more there is the better, but any piece of furniture looks better if it is smoothed with glasspaper and given several coats of paint.

Many useful hints are given in a BBC publication, *How to Form a Playgroup*, obtainable from the BBC and from bookshops or newsagents.

As a general principle furniture and other apparatus should be robust: children can be remarkably destructive. On the other hand, if the apparatus has to be set out and cleared away daily, then lightness of weight must be aimed at, especially as it is probably women who will have to do most of the coolie work. In this case, well-greased and free-running caster wheels should be fitted.

Where part of a house is to be used as a permanent or semi-permanent playgroup, then it may be possible to earmark different rooms for different purposes. This has something to recommend it: noisy activities or those that are wet and messy can be kept away from quiet ones. On the other hand it means that the leader cannot monitor all the activities that are going on. Where there are experienced assistants this is of little account, but if, through illness, say, the assistant is away, the attempt to keep an eye on what is going on in two or three rooms, a corridor, washroom and the garden can be very exhausting. Where two or three rooms are available then it is probably better to have two or three self-contained groups, each with a leader or assistant in charge. This will lead to some duplication of apparatus which is not necessarily a bad thing, as each child will have easier and more frequent access to different activities. In this case story-time corner and the Wendy house may have to be confined to a corridor and some time-sharing arrangement reached for each group.

Where more than one class is in operation, there should be no attempt at dividing the children up into age groups, with the younger children in one group and the older in another. A more workable system is 'family-grouping' as practised in many LEA infants' schools. Here each class contains a group of children ready to move on to the junior class, another group of new entrants and a third in the middle. There are some minor disadvantages in this: stories that the older children like may be a little too sophisticated for the youngest, while those for the latter group may be too babyish for the 'fives'. These disadvantages are more apparent than real. Children are conservative: the older ones like to return to the stories they know and love, and the differences in understanding between three- and five-year-olds are not always so great. If it is felt necessary to divide the children for any activity, this can be easily arranged in the generally informal atmosphere that is found in most playgroups. In any case the advantages far outweigh the disadvantages. New children who may be tearful and shy gain confidence from seeing other children busily playing and working away. The class is always 'ongoing'. The children who have been there before know what is expected of them and what they may expect from the teacher and each other. New entrants come into a stable situation and there is no need to re-create a new one every year. Then again older children can often be seen helping younger ones, taking down and hanging up a towel in the washroom, showing them where the lavatories are and so on. From the point of view of the teacher there is a hidden advantage. Where older and younger children are together there will be no temptation to try 'class teaching'. The teaching that does go on will be individual or in small groups, where the teacher can give every child more individual attention and can plan her intervention into the process of development with each child's personal strengths and weaknesses in mind.

It is more probable that most playgroups will use a large church hall or similar room. Even though apparatus may have to be tidied away at the end of every afternoon there are some advantages in this. The space can be used for the activities that the leader wants: she will be able to use more space for one activity and less for another and so on. There are advantages too in having a large room divided up by low partitions. A four-foot set of shelves is very much like a wall to a little child, but the leader can see over it and more easily keep an eye on every activity that is going on.

Since each playgroup will probably occupy a different shape and size of premises, no useful purpose would be served in drawing up hypothetical plans. Each leader and committee will have to make their own plans, taking into account the numbers of children involved, the adults available, the sort of apparatus that they have and the kinds of activities they want to encourage. However, space for the following activities is essential:

  sand and water play
  building, using large blocks and boxes
  home corner/Wendy house
  reading/quiet corner
  a workbench
  space for table-bound activities
  space for moving activities (whether planned in movement
    sessions, or unplanned, individual playing with toy cars,
    etc.)

The first four of these can usefully be fitted into corners each one shut off, if necessary by shelves or screens. The 'building corner' may not need this, but some form of limitation is valuable: it stops more robust activities from overlapping into the building area and perhaps interfering with some carefully thought out construction, or the construction may achieve gargantuan proportions, taking limited space away from other activities.

These activities suggest their own sorts of apparatus. Sand and water play demand appropriate trays, with buckets to fill the water tray. Brooms, mops and dustpans and buckets will be needed for cleaning up. It may be possible to use the ones provided by the hall, but this should be checked first. If the group has to supply its own cleaning tools then they should be clearly marked and locked away after use. The reading corner can be marked off by a set of folding shelves on which are displayed gaily coloured books in good condition. If the shelves have to be put away every day they should be hinged to fold in half and be mounted on runners. The floor of the quiet area should be covered with a square of carpet, it is useful to have things to sit on such as cushions or low stools. There should be one comfortable chair for the adult to sit in as well! Books may be purchased. Some bookshops and publishers give discounts on books sold to schools. Enquiries should be made locally about this. Most public libraries, either locally or on a county basis, supply books to schools and see that they are changed regularly for new ones. Many libraries also have on their staff at least one specialist in children's books. If there is one locally she should be asked for advice as to what is suitable.

Every playgroup should obtain a real miniature work bench, complete with vice and real tenon saw, screwdrivers, hammer and nails. The tools must be *real*. Little children are surprisingly careful and if they miss with the hammer it's a useful lesson! The saw usually gets blunted and although it is less dangerous will not actually cut wood. It may be possible to buy off-cuts of balsa wood from a do-it-yourself or model shop. This can be cut easily and used for making ships, planes and whatever. They may not look much like ships and planes but that is not important. What is important is the original idea, and the way in which it is carried out. In addition rough measuring (by eye) and skills in manipulation are practised. It is often best to keep the work bench in a corner near the leader or an assistant. Some initial demonstration of care in using the saw is essential, thereafter the children should be left to their own devices.

The home corner or Wendy house may be stocked with a cooker, ironing board, chairs, bed table, dressing-up clothes and so on. It is here that the children often play out different adult roles: now mother or father (sex is, for the youngest children, often irrelevant: sex-typing of roles enters later), doctor, nurse or washerwoman. It can be marked off by a semi-permanent frame of wood covered with hardboard and gaily painted. In this case there is usually a proper, hinged door and a window. Where no permanent structure is possible an acceptable substitute can be made with a clothes-horse, covered with bright material or hessian. Two such screens can be drawn round the home corner to create a make-believe world of home.

In addition to these 'corners' (which may or may not be actual *corners*) space is needed for table-bound activities. It is usually better to keep different activities separated on different tables: one for the paint and messy work, another for the constructional toys and jig-saws, a third for matching games, and so on. The tables are low and there must be an adequate number of chairs of a suitable height for all the children. It is better to have several extra. Some get broken and the children need to sit while they are being repaired. When future new entrants visit the class they will need to be

able to find a seat. By the same token there will be a need for
several adult-size chairs. A number of low cupboards are
essential for materials to be stored in. If these have to be put
away daily then they too should be as light as is consistent
with security and should be mounted on wheels. It is better if
they can be left permanently out where they will be needed,
but this must be negotiated in advance with the owners. If
they are left out they should be very strongly built and fitted
with a stout, good-quality padlock. Other users of the hall
will be inquisitive and with the best will in the world material
will become damaged, lost or mislaid. Optimism about
robustness will be dispelled by seeing twenty or thirty scouts
playing 'British bulldog'.

Finally there must be space to move in. Sometimes this
will be used for music and movement sessions, at others for
playing with cars and trains, building roads of planks, and so
on. If it is impossible to have climbing frames outside then it
may be necessary to set out (and later tidy away) indoor
climbing apparatus, similar to that used for PE in infants'
schools. Some of this may be obtainable from the LEA, but
much will probably have to be bought. If it is made at home
then it must be well made. Great care must be taken to
ensure that is does not collapse or that the children do not
get splinters from unfinished materials. An additional
problem with this movable material is that extra storage
space will be needed. Where a public hall is used it is
probably this question of storage space that will be the most
serious limiting factor.

Planning the day
Every teacher will want to plan her own day so that children
can experience a full range of activities. There is something to
be said for the excitement of abandoning the regular
programme on the spur of the moment: perhaps one blustery
day in autumn to go to the park where there is plenty of
room for the children to whirl around in the wind like the
leaves. Dead, brown, crackly leaves can be gathered. Some of
these the teacher will make into a decoration, others the
children will use in their collage. There are abundant
opportunities for the teacher to tell simply the facts of

autumnal life, and when the children return to school she can find suitable songs and stories with an autumnal theme. Or a walk by the canal one frosty morning can be full of delight to children. On the other hand the programme should not be chaotic: one of the advantages of playgroups in the sphere of social training is the stability and regularity they offer to the child. It is the child who varies; the background, for much of the time, should not change. So it is useful to have a regular framework into which the different activities can be slotted.

To the beginner the day seems terribly long. How will she be able to fill it? I remember feeling much the same when I was training as a teacher and many of my students have subsequently reported a similar worry. Actually this worry is baseless. Very soon after starting to teach, at whatever level, the problem becomes the opposite: how can I fit in all the things that I must do and that I want to do? What, if anything, must be left out? In the first place, within any school day there are some activities that must occur and these occupy a lot of time. At the nursery and infant level they tend to take up even more time. Going to the lavatory, washing your hands and noticing the bubbles formed by soapy water, putting on your shoes and trying hard to do up the laces yourself: all these take much time. Then again children, especially little children, work much more slowly than many adults without experience imagine. Children are, too, a timeless bunch (in many cases an accurate sense of the passage of time may not fully develop until well on into the secondary stage). If a child is washing his hands and something catches his attention, it will occupy his whole being. He forgets his wet dripping hands and the teacher waiting to tell a story or mother wanting to take him home. He is lost for the time being in a very different world. Finally, small children do not need a constantly changing stimulus. Even older children (and probably young adults, too) do not. Because adult and secondary education tends to be syllabus-bound — today we do 'X', next lesson it will be 'Y' and next week 'Z' — many teachers and other adults try to conceive of early education in the same way.

Actually it does not work, even with adults. I frequently ask classes of keen, experienced teachers just how much they remembered from the two or three lectures in which they had explained to them, during their initial training, the main ideas of Piaget's important work on the intellectual development of young children. Most admit that they retained very little. They needed time to think about the new ideas, to have experience with children, to return to the subject and read and think again, to ask their tutors questions and worry out the answers for themselves. Now the work of Piaget is difficult; but so are the problems that we set children and the things that we expect of them to absorb. That they are easy for the teacher does not mean that they are at all easy for the child. If student teachers are to benefit from being exposed to the work of Piaget they must struggle with it themselves until they have absorbed it, that is until they have assimilated it and accommodated themselves to it. This takes time. No lecturer can short-circuit this process. The same applies to children, but to an even greater degree because they are less sophisticated. We say that little children are conservative, that they 'like to return to the old things'. Most of us like to relax occasionally and do things that do not stretch us too much. Children are the same, but the returning to familiar stories and activities has another additional, and probably more important cause: the story or activity is still exercising the children in some way. There is something they have not yet got into perspective or have not yet fully understood. When they have absorbed it completely, when it no longer poses a problem, then they will leave it and move onwards. For most of us education and progress is not a continuous line that leads from A to B. It is more like the yellow brick road in *The Wizard of Oz*, it loops back on itself now and again. But it never covers exactly the same ground: we merely look at the old scenery from a new vantage point.

Let us try to sketch out a possible half-day programme in a nursery class or playgroup.

Staff arrive and begin to set out apparatus   8.50 – 9.00

Most children arrive   9.30

INDIVIDUAL PLAY—
activities carefully selected by playgroup leader   9.30 — 10.30

Milk, put on outside clothing   10.30

FREE PLAY OUTSIDE OR INDOORS,
or MUSIC AND MOVEMENT   10.45 — 11.15

STORY, FINGER GAMES, NURSERY
RHYME or CHILDREN TALKING   11.15 — 12.00

Parents arrive to collect children, staff tidy
room and prepare apparatus for the afternoon
session   12.00 — 12.30

Staff lunch and free time   12.30 — 1.30

Children begin to arrive for afternoon session   1.30

Repeat of the morning

We see from this sketch that the children's 'day' falls into three major activities: *directed choice play*, *movement or free-choice play*, *story*. The music and movement session has been briefly described elsewhere as have many of the activities in the free-choice sessions. Of course these sessions are not at all free choice, strictly speaking. The freedom of choice is strictly limited to what the playgroup provides and the teacher plans. This applies in any playgroup or nursery class even where the teachers believe they are not influencing the children in any way. Let us accept that we *are* going to influence them, and do it a little more efficiently.

The principal idea underlying this book is that teachers must influence their young pupils more consciously and purposefully than has been hitherto common in pre-school settings. How is this to be achieved? Mainly by setting up interesting and exciting activities that will really engage each child, then by making sure that *every* child is led to experiment a little further. The teacher may make a comment about something the child has done or is doing. She may ask him a question or suggest doing it another way. Every child should receive some personal attention every day. Once the child gets to the infants' school and junior school with classes of thirty, thirty-five or even forty children his chances of a bit of unshared adult attention diminish rapidly. If we divide the time available by the number of children per teacher, then we may find that even if the teacher were to devote her attention exclusively to this activity, each child would not receive more than three or four minutes to himself in any one day. If we assume that there are two 'business' hours in a playgroup session in which the teacher can properly be expected to be striving to do her utmost, with a ratio of eight children to every adult, then each child should be able to receive on the average fifteen minutes of time daily. Now the research suggests that a little and often is better with young children than a big dose of experience all in one go. Thus the aim should be for the teacher to spend a few minutes talking to and listening to each child daily in each 'half' of the session. During this period she makes suggestions, gives reinforcement and generally makes the child feel important to herself and to the group. It is little enough but probably sufficient. If it does not happen this time it will never happen again during formal education until the child gets into the sixth form of a good grammar school or to university (and it is rare enough even there).

Let us see how this may be achieved. First the teacher plans what activities will be available to the children during the free-choice periods. In addition to the Wendy house, building blocks, sand and water trays and work bench, which are always there, let us assume that materials will be laid out on the tables before the children arrive. One table will have, say, construction toys and dough-plasticine, another pre-number matching games and jig-saws. Around these the assistants will hover unobtrusively (at first). They will help the children to choose some activity that is fitted to their stage of development, will start them off and have a word with each of them. The third table will be devoted to a new activity that the leader wishes to introduce, say finger painting, which she knows that a group of her pupils have not tried before. As the children come in they will distribute

themselves over all the activities as they wish, some working
with the sand and water, others playing out social roles in the
Wendy house and so on. Gradually the leader attracts the
attention of the children she wants to introduce to the new
activity. They put on their aprons or 'backwards shirts' and
set to. The leader shows something of what can be done and
lets the children experiment. They talk about textures and
colours and how the paste feels under their fingers. After a
while the leader will melt away, keeping·an eye on the
activity from a distance while she talks to other children.
Some of the children will tire or lose interest. Their work is
hung up to dry, perhaps over a radiator, or with pegs on a
piece of string strung across one corner of the room. The
children go to wash their hands. When all have finished some
of the bigger ones help to wipe the tables down and clear up.
Later that activity, no longer new, can be set out as a
standard activity which some children will choose freely,
others not.

At this time another new activity, perhaps 'matching snap'
is introduced, this time with a slightly older group. In this
way, most children are given freedom, but each child makes
steady progress towards mastering new skills, while being able
to return whenever he wishes to the previous activities he has
already enjoyed. The secret is never to introduce too much
new all at once. If this is done then one risks having twenty
or thirty little children all demanding attention at the same
time. We have all seen queues of children in a normal class
waiting to gain the teacher's attention: perhaps to take a turn
at reading, to have sums marked, to ask how a word is spelled
or whatever. In part this is inevitable with oversize classes,
but it also suggests a faulty organisation. It is possible to
arrange things so that most children are working on 'con-
solidation' activities, practising skills they have mastered,
while one group is meeting something new and needing
attention from the teacher. For children to stand in a queue
is a waste of their time, and time is valuable. It also suggests
that they have not been taught to make intelligent guesses
(perhaps because guesses have been marked wrong in the past
and the child punished or ridiculed) or to find some other
activity. Some children are like some adults: it is easier to

stand and chat to our friends than to do any work. If the teacher allows us to stand around and waste time then why shouldn't we?

There should be no call for children in nursery classes and playgroups to stand around idly. Fortunately little children tend to be very busy and very curious people. They are always on the go – as many a worn-out mother has discovered. Playgroup leaders can take advantage of this and with care can help their pupils to take increasing responsibility themselves for the fruitful direction of their own activities. It is not an accident of nature that some children are always busily creative and others apathetic. Other things being equal it is that these very different children have had different experiences that have made them view the world and their place in it from very different angles. By judicious use of praise (that is, reinforcement), by encouraging their pupils to make a reasonable 'shot' – at their own level and in their own terms – at solving problems, by talking about their answers and by helping them to acquire essential basic skills, the teachers will help the young children in their charge to channel their curiosity and busy-ness along socially approved and personally fruitful lines. If a playgroup or nursery class is organised along the lines set out in this book it is very probable that most of their pupils will always be able to find something useful to do. The world is full of interesting things and ideas. Each year and each month brings still more new and interesting things and ideas. The babies of today will have to acquire vast bodies of information and to master many skills undreamed of by their grandparents. To do this takes time and time is limited. Let us not waste it.

Epilogue

When one reads the literature on the early education of young children one is struck by the amount of sheer dishonest thinking involved. Largely under the influence of psychoanalytic theorising and with little or no actual supporting evidence, teachers of the very young appear to have abdicated from their role. The most widespread view seems to be: 'Be patient, be nice, don't push, let the child play.' One American writer, Barbara Biber, has written: 'Children, at all levels, pool their ideas in free dramatic play, expose each other to new impressions, stimulate each other to new wondering and questioning. Can we fail to recognise this process as learning?' Of course it is learning, and it does occur, but for how many children? Do all children do this or is it only a few? My own observations of many nursery classes suggest that many children engage in rather repetitive activities, following the lead of a few more adventurous souls. We know that only children, brought up in the company of adults, seem to develop more rapidly than children with many brothers and sisters. Children from small families tend to do better than those from large families, largely apparently because they get more attention and stimulation from adults. In an extreme case there are reports of twins who grew up mainly in each other's company: they developed their own private language and were quite seriously retarded.

The books that teachers, students and parents buy abound in examples of the apparently spontaneous creativity of young children: they have ideas and exchange them, they solve problems and build elaborate constructions all without any intervention by the teacher. It all seems very impressive. Should an outsider express scepticism? If real examples are given have we the right to be suspicious? Rarely can we bring forward any evidence to support our suspicions, but I was able to carry out a rough statistical analysis of the various activities described in one popular book by an infants' headmistress of long experience.

It was found that, in all, 172 examples of spontaneous creativity were described. These were attributed to 76 different children. Now we cannot know how many children passed through the school but indirect evidence suggests that these 76 children formed *at most* one-fifth of the total, and possibly only one-tenth. Perhaps all the other children did equally creative things, but our suspicions are aroused when we realise that over one-third of the bright ideas quoted came from only 12 children, and one boy alone was responsible for no fewer than 12! Few descriptions were given of the children involved, but indirect evidence suggests that most came from middle-class homes.

We know that many middle-class parents encourage their children to explore, to discuss, to experiment and so on. If this is the case, were the apparent successes in the school due, not so much to the emphasis laid on freedom by the headmistress, but to the activities of the parents before the children ever came to school? What were the other eighty per cent of the children doing while the creative twenty per cent were being noticed by the headmistress? It is not surprising that cynics often claim that middle-class parents favour freedom in education, because they make sure that their children learn the important basic essentials at home. Teachers must observe *all* their pupils. They must not be content with noticing the activities of the brightest and then fool themselves that all the children are being equally creative.

We find ourselves, then, in a strange situation. Controlled research shows that, other things being equal, the benefits gained from this early experience seem to disappear by middle or late childhood. Yet, in spite of this, all the experts insist that we need more of this early education. In the Plowden Report we can find both of these views clearly expressed:

> There is a wide measure of agreement among informed observers that nursery provision on a substantial scale is

desirable, not only on educational grounds, but also for social, health and welfare considerations (para.296).

The research evidence so far available is both *too sparse* and too heavily weighted by studies of special groups of children *to be decisively in* favour of nursery education for all (para.303).

The educational performance of children from the nursery schools was higher at eight than that of other children, but the advantage was lost by eleven, and at fifteen they did slightly less well than their contemporaries. In no year, however, were the differences statistically significant. *Maladjustment among children who had attended nurseries was higher than amongst other children* (para.302). (*Children in their Primary Schools*, A Report for the Central Advisory Council for Education (England), HMSO, London, 1966.)

There may be reasons for this higher incidence of maladjustment, especially since some of the children were admitted to nursery classes because of early symptoms of maladjustment: 'Children may have been admitted to nursery schools because of problems of behaviour' (para.302), but one wonders why these children have *not* benefited from the advantages of 'opportunities for play both indoors and out, the companionship of other children and the presence of understanding adults which nursery education provides' claimed by the Nursery Schools Association in support of their demand for more nursery places (para.398).

The Plowden Committee relies 'therefore, on the overwhelming evidence of experienced educators' (para.303) and believes that the case for increased nursery education is a strong one (para.296).

On the one hand we find a body of experts urging us to spend ever-increasing sums of money on nursery education and to expose increased numbers of children to it, while on the other hand there is no evidence that the experience has any lasting influence educationally, and may do actual harm to some of the children.

How can we explain this paradox? In the first place very few educational situations, especially those involving very young children, have built-in objective evaluation processes. The only person who judges whether the situation is or is not successful is the one who is emotionally and professionally committed to maintaining that situation. When outsiders, like administrators, psychologists and laymen-parents query what is being done, they are put firmly in their place by the experts. (Incidentally one of the roots of 'modern maths' was a horrified recognition by some professional mathematicians of what was being taught to their children. They decided to look into the problems of teaching maths themselves and thereby initiated a recolution.)

We have seen that the opinions of some of the experts in the field may have been distorted by a tendency to notice only the successful children, whereas what is needed is an objective assessment of the gains and losses by *all* children. Needless to say the research that highlights the lack of success of much pre-school education is based on the results of observations made on large numbers of children. This may explain to some extent the discrepancy between the research and the views of 'experts', but it is probably not the whole story. Part of the difference surely arises' from the fact that the experts have taken what is only a *means*, albeit a very necessary means, that is freedom to play, and made it an *end*.

The most likely outcome will be that if, in spite of the unsatisfactory results of much pre-school education as currently practised, the advice of the leading exponents is followed we will merely extend the 'mixture as before' to a wider circle of children. More money will be spent with little, if any, real gain to the children involved. Now, it may be that other benefits can be gained from setting up playgroups and nursery schools. Some of these have been outlined in *Our Young Children* (published by HMSO for the Department of Health and Social Security, and several other government departments). Here we read: 'In some ways modern living militates against the interests of young children.' The reasons advanced include blocks of high-rise flats and houses without gardens, where space is restricted and noise may be un-welcome; mothers working, or unable, because of mental or physical handicap, to care for their children; separation as a result of rehousing schemes of young families from older relatives, fatherless families. These are serious problems and they must be as far as possible overcome. But let us be honest: if playgroups and nursery classes are set up for these reasons and in the absence of evidence of actual *educational* benefit, then we are no longer talking about education. We are merely trying to ameliorate the consequences of current marital breakdown, of the short-sightedness of town and country planners and administrators and of the consequences of economic advance with its insatiable demand for increased numbers of workers. If we set up nursery groups for these reasons then it probably does not much matter what goes on, so long as the children are cared for and kept out of danger. Nursery teachers are reduced to the status of child-minders.

In contrast to that bleak picture, the idea underlying this book is that the education of young children can have positive results. It can do far more than merely offset some of the more unwelcome side effects of modern life. It can help children to prepare for a more fruitful and richer personal life in later years, and perhaps, by this means, it may contribute to the future elimination of some of these unwelcome aspects. But education is more than merely a preparation for a satisfying and full adult life. It must also engender satisfaction while it is in progress. Observation and experience suggest that, like adults, children are not unhappy when they are busily engaged in and mastering some stimulating and challenging activity. Unhappiness often stems from a lack of purpose, from boredom and from a dull repetition of stereotyped activities.

This suggests that the teacher or playgroup leader must be prepared to play a more dynamic part in the group of children under her care than merely to provide interesting activities, hold the ring in childish squabbles and bandage up a grazed knee. She must abandon the view quoted earlier: 'Be patient, be nice, don't push, let the child play.' Formal education is an artificial and planned intervention into natural development with the specific intention of speeding up this development and making it more efficient through eliminating unnecessary errors. Even under the best conditions education is a lengthy process. 'The most elementary and apparently the most self-evident ideas need a long and difficult elaboration,' wrote Jean Piaget in *Psychology and Epistemology*. Our education is probably never completed until we die, and some would hold that it continues thereafter. The contribution of the early years may appear to some unreflecting people to be rather vague and minimal. The sixth-former studying calculus or reading French literature, the undergraduate exploring new fields of computers or sociology, the student engineer studying the construction of bridges may all appear more glamorous. Certainly they attract more public money and enjoy high esteem. The contribution they make to society may appear more obvious and striking. But none of these can occur without an adequate foundation gained in early childhood. In addition only a small minority of people (in Britain at any rate) actually go on to benefit from these advanced studies. Rather than admire the few we ought to be concerned about the many who do not reach the heights. The failure of the majority to do so may be due to personal and social inadequacies, but an increasing number of psychologists are coming to believe that it may be due more to *inadequacies of early experience*. Change this early experience in certain positive, clearly planned ways and who knows where we may end? In *The Organisation of Behaviour* Donald Hebb has written: 'The country may be full of potential geniuses, for all we know, and it should be a pressing concern for psychology to discover the conditions that will develop whatever potentialities a child may have.'

Early childhood is the most important period of our life. It is at this time that the bases of our social, personal and intellectual habits, assumptions and values are laid down. They may be changed in later life, but as we grow older the possibilities of change become increasingly restricted, and any change demands more effort on our parts. During the early years children seem not only to learn more rapidly but what they learn is often more permanent and resistant to subsequent change.

It seems therefore a pity to allow these children to spend their important early years in ill-conceived activities that not only do not have much lasting influence but that may also do positive harm. Nor should education in these years be regarded or justified on purely non-educational grounds. Early childhood is the time for learning, among other things, and if extended pre-school education is to be justified educationally then the function of the teacher is to set up situations in which all her pupils can actually learn. There is a danger in the emphasis which I am urging here. If teachers are urged to take a more positive stand there is a danger that they will see their new function as impelling them to teach. If the lessons of this book are forgotten (that whatever a teacher does, it is *the pupil who must learn*, that in the final analysis no one can really teach anything to anyone else, that the learner learns by constructing his own personal models on the basis of applying a limited set of intellectual processes to sets of experiences) then there will be formal teaching. This would be disastrous at this early age. Indeed it would probably be advantageous to delay formal work for most children until the age of seven or so, but only if the years between three and seven are filled with really meaningful educational activity along the lines suggested in this book.

Although this view places the learner right in the centre of the educational process it by no means undervalues the teacher: she is the most important educator that the child will ever encounter. She must be well educated herself and she must be able to structure the educational experiences so that they are appropriate to the children in her care.

Jerome Bruner has claimed, probably truthfully, that any topic can be taught in an intellectually meaningful and respectable way to children of any age, so long as it is presented in a form appropriate to the learner. He quotes a striking example, taken from physics:

A quite young child can plainly act on the basis of the 'principles' of a balance beam, and indicates that he can do so by being able to handle himself on a see-saw. He knows that to get his side to go down farther he has to move out from the centre. A somewhat older child can represent the balance beam to himself either by a model on which rings can be hung and balanced or by a drawing . . . Finally, a balance beam can be described in ordinary English . . . or it can be even better described mathematically by reference to Newton's Law of Moments (*Toward a Theory of Instruction*, p.45).

In this example we see that the same principles can be taught and used at three different levels, each appropriate to the age and abilities of the learner.

In order to achieve this new style of early education, new and probably great demands must be made on the teacher. First she must seek to construct an environment in which all children can gain personal and social confidence and in which an experimental approach to learning is seen as natural. She must, within this environment, observe every child and at the key moment encourage him to move on from one activity which is no longer stretching him to another at a higher level or to one that will extend his thinking along new dimensions. She must always be ready to step in with encouragement when the child is making heavy weather, and with praise and other reinforcement when some new skill has been mastered or an old skill has been applied in a new direction. At the appropriate moment she must give each child the necessary linguistic experience to enable him to express his new knowledge symbolically, to communicate it to others and to understand their communications. But perhaps her greatest problem 'is to keep out of the way, to prevent [herself] from becoming a perennial source of information, interfering with the child's ability to take over the role of being his own corrector' ibid. p.70).

None of this denies the value of freedom. Children must have freedom to play and experiment, which are in any case much the same in early infancy. We know that advanced learning can be built only on a sound foundation of wide and rich experience. We know too that in the last analysis teachers cannot teach little children very much: they can only set up situations that allow and encourage the children to learn. To try to speed up learning by the too early introduction of formal work and lessons often results in long-term failure and dislike of the whole process of education, even though it may seem to work in the short run. Freedom, then, is necessary. But it is not sufficient. Most children will not educate themselves in the total absence of adult help. A totally free system means that essential experience may occur randomly, at an inappropriate time, or perhaps even not at all. Teaching should be seen as a planned intervention in the learning process that occurs in order to make the learning more efficient and more rapid. Such intervention must have as its aim the progress of all the children, not merely the stimulation of the lucky few. This intervention must be delicate. It must depend on personal sensitivity and knowledge on the part of the teacher, who must know how children think and how they learn, how they grow and why they sometimes seem to stand still.

Perhaps then the greatest need for the teacher of young children especially is a sense of timing: knowing when to intervene and when to let the children be doing. In much pre-school education as currently practised there is a great tendency to leave the children too much to their own resources. The teacher is urged to intervene more purposefully, but not excessively. Little direct advice can be given about this except:

Wait on the child. Let experience precede words. Let this experience be rich, varied and extensive. Then intervene.

Good luck!

Postscript

In all the known history of mankind, advances have been made primarily in physical technology; in the capacity of handling the inanimate world about Man. Control of self and society has been left to chance or vague gropings of intuitive ethical systems based on inspiration and emotion.

Isaac Asimov, *Second Foundation*

Appendix

1 *National organisations concerned with pre-school education:*

    Nursery School Association
    Montgomery Hall
    Harleyford Street
    Kennington Oval
    London SE11   telephone 01—582 8744

    Pre-School Playgroups Association
    Alford House
    Aveline Street
    London SE11   telephone 01—582 8871

    Save the Children Fund
    29 Queen Anne's Gate
    London SW1   telephone 01—930 2461

2 *Suppliers of educational toys and materials:*

    Community Playthings
    Robertsbridge
    Sussex

    ESA School Materials Division
    Pinnacles
    P O Box 22
    Harlow
    Essex CM19 5AY

Goodwood Playthings
Chichester
Sussex

Hope Educational
Ashtons Mill
Chapeltown Street
Manchester M1 2NH

James Galt Ltd
Brookfield Road
Cheadle
Cheshire

Philip & Tacey Ltd
Andover
Hampshire

Three-Four-Five Ltd
33 West Hill
London SW18 1 RP

3 *Organisations concerned with the needs of special groups of children:*

Association for Special Education
19 Hamilton Road
Wallasey
Cheshire L45 9JE   telephone 051—525 3451

National Association for Gifted Children
27 John Adam Street
London WC2N 6HX   telephone 01—930 7731

National Association for Mental Health
39 Queen Anne Street
London W1M 0A5   telephone 01—935 1272

National Association for Mental Health in Children
86 Newman Street
London W1P 4AR   telephone 01—636 2861

National Association for Remedial Education
9 Cranleigh Rise
Eaton
Norwich NOR 54D   telephone 0603 56624

National Froebel Foundation
Froebel Institute
Grove House
Roehampton Lane
London SW15 5PJ   telephone 01—878 3489

National Society for Autistic Children
1A Golders Green Road
London NW11 8EA   telephone 01—458 4375

Nursery Nurses Examinations Board
13 Grosvenor Place
London SW1X 7EN   telephone 01—235 9961

Royal National Institute for the Blind
224 Great Portland Street
London W1N 6AA   telephone 01—387 5251

Royal National Institute of the Deaf
105 Gower Street
London WC1E 6AH   telephone 01—387 8033

The Spastics Society
12 Park Crescent
London W1N 4EQ   telephone 01—636 5020

The Workers' Educational Association
Temple House
9 Upper Berkeley Street
London W1H 8BY   telephone 01—402 5608

4 *Some useful books*

(a) General background reading:
John and Elizabeth Newson, *Patterns of Infant Care*, 1965
    Pelican. *Four Years Old in an Urban Community*, 1970
    Pelican.
R.H. Anderson and H.G. Shane, *As the Twig is Bent:
    Readings in Early Childhood Education*, 1971 Houghton
    Mifflin. (A collection of readings, some of which are
    excellent and represent the best of modern thinking in
    early education. Especially important are chapters 5, 6, 7,
    12, 13, 19, 22, 26, 27.)
J. Holt, *How Children Fail*, 1969 Pelican.

(b) Books on play:
E.M. Matterson, *Play with a Purpose for Under-Sevens*, 1965
    Penguin.
S. Millar, *The Psychology of Play*, 1968 Pelican.

(c) Books on special topics:
Frank Smith, *Understanding Reading*, 1972 Holt, Rinehart
    & Winston. (Probably the best book on the subject. It is
    one of the most readable, up to date accounts of modern
    cognitive psychology and linguistics.)
M. Holt and Z. Dienes, *Let's Play Maths*, 1971 Penguin. (Full
    of excellent ideas and explanations.)
R.R. Skemp, *The Psychology of Learning Mathematics*, 1971
    Pelican. (Another excellent book for the serious reader. It
    is none the less simply written, and also has many very
    useful and suggestive ideas.)
Nuffield Foundation, *The First Three Years*, 1970 W. and
    R. Chambers and John Murray. (This is the first intro-
    ductory book of a whole series. The authors write: 'But
    "setting the children free" does not mean starting a riot
    with a room full of junk for ammunition. The changeover
    to the new approach brings its own problems. The guide *I
    do and I understand* — which is of a different character
    from the others — faces these problems and attempts to
    show how they can be overcome.')

(d) The other books fall into three categories:
Teachers' guides
These cover three main topics: Computation and structure; shape and size; graphs leading to algebra.

These books do not cover 'years' but themes, which are met over and over again at different levels of complexity.

Weaving guides
These are 'single-concept' books, with detailed instructions and information about one subject.

Check-up guides
The intention here is to avoid the common kinds of 'tests' and replace them by individual check-ups for individual children to see whether they have really constructed their own mathematical concepts.

These books have been written with a very practical aim for teachers of children of infant and junior age. They are full of useful, practical suggestions, together with explanations of why some ways might be better than others. They contain many examples of children's work, which the authors urge us to look upon 'as an example of work that children might produce rather than a model of work they should produce'. It is the teacher who decides what will be done and who guides the individual child towards improving his own standards of self-evaluation.

The books contain not only direct teaching suggestions but examples of apparently un-mathematical subjects and situations which can be used to develop a mathematical sense.

Pre-school Playgroup Association, Bath and district branch, *40 Action Songs, 40 Finger Plays*. This excellent little work is obtainable from the Pre-Schools Playgroups Association.

Edith Fowke, *Sally Go Round the Sun*, 1969 McLelland & Stewart, Toronto (300 nursery songs from Canada).

E. Matterson, *The Little Puffin—Nursery Songs and Rhymes* 1962 Puffin.

D. Mitchell and C. Blyton, *Faber Book of Nursery Songs*, 1968 Faber.
I. and P. Opie, *Oxford Dictionary of Nursery Rhymes*, 1951 Oxford University Press.

Acknowledgments

The author gratefully acknowledges the help of his children who taught him more than anything or anyone else about young people, of Dorothea Brooke who read his manuscript and made many useful comments, of Ken Duncan for his photographic skills and of Rosalind Blackmore who typed the manuscript in an heroic race against time.

The publishers' permission to quote from the following works is gratefully acknowledged:
Barbara Biber, *The Role of Play,* Vassar Quarterly
J.S. Bruner, *Toward A Theory of Instruction*, Harvard University Press
J. Gay and M. Cole, *The New Mathematics and an Old Culture*, Holt, Rinehart & Winston
F. Smith, *Understanding Reading*, Holt, Rinehart & Winston.
D.O. Hebb, *The Organisation of Behaviour*, Wiley & Sons
R.A. Skemp, *The Psychology of Learning Maths*, Penguin
The Nuffield Junior Mathematics Project, W. & R. Chambers/ John Murray
Mathematics in Primary Schools, Children and their Primary Schools, Our Young Children, all published by HMSO.
Isaac Asimov, *Second Foundation*, Doubleday

The staff and children of the ULU Playgroup are thanked for allowing themselves to be photographed.